PRAISE FOR
HERO TO ZERO

"In his typical raw, rough and real style, Zach Fortier brings another page-turner of a book! A realistic look inside the lives of the people that carry a badge, and what happens when they tarnish it."
• Ashley Fontainne
Award-winning Author of "Number Seventy-Five" •

"I found *Hero to Zero* to be a compelling read and it provides unbelievable insights into "cop life." It reaffirms the myth about the secrecy and confidentiality inside the brotherhood of blue—it does exist even if on an expiry date."
• Eager Reader •

"…an interesting account of those in uniform whom most of us look up to, look to for help, look to for guidance, and wouldn't ever imagine acting in any way like those they are protecting us from. This book gives us the inside scoop in the no-nonsense way that Zach sees life around him and is written in that same no-nonsense way."
• Greatreader •

"The stories are each fascinating in their own way, as are the behind-the-scenes details of life in law enforcement. Fortier has put out another excellent work with this book."
• Holly Cochran •

"The stories are gritty, told in a personal and conversational manner. It feels like you're chatting over a beer or something, which makes it a quick and enjoyable read."
• S. Boddie •

HERO TO ZERO

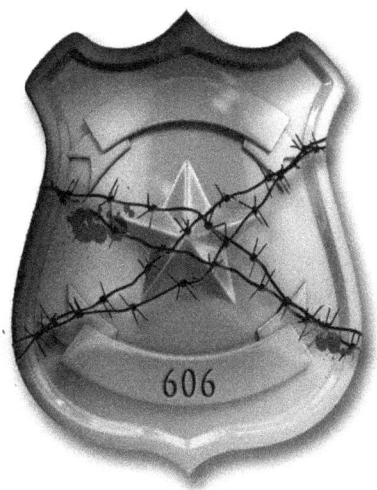

ZACH FORTIER

steeleshark
press

Published by
SteeleShark Press

ISBN-13: 978-0615914367
ISBN-10: 0615914365

Visit the author at:
Website: *www.zachfortier.com*
Blog: *www.authorzachfortier.blogspot.com*
Facebook: *www.facebook.com/authorzach.fortier*
Twitter: *www.twitter.com/zachfortier1*
Goodreads: *www.goodreads.com/author/show/5164780.Zach_Fortier*

ALSO BY ZACH FORTIER

CURBCHEK

STREET CREDS

CURBCHEK RELOAD

LANDED ON BLACK
COMING SOON

CHAPTER ONE
ROBERT SUGGS

DURING THE 1980S, I WAS working as a military cop. It was a time of nuclear protests and people were nowhere near as pro-military as they are today. People hated you instantly if you were in the military. To be a military cop was the lowest of lows, the bottom of the military shit pile. This was where I met Robert Suggs.

He was a military cop as I was, but he was very different from the rest of us. He embraced the "cop lifestyle" with a zeal that was somehow intoxicating. He had a passion for being a cop that was unheard of in the environment of the military. Everyone else who wore the uniform looked down on us. Suggs brushed all the criticism aside and looked upon being a cop as a worthwhile pursuit—a calling. He saw it as something to devote your life to and never feel ashamed of. His passion was feverish.

He not only worked as a military cop, sometimes sixty hours or more a week (we all worked long, long hours due to staffing levels being at bare minimums), he also volunteered as a reserve police officer for the Spokane Police Department. He lived breathed and ate *cop*, 24 hours a day, seven days a week.

I started to talk to Suggs on night shift when our patrols would overlap. I made it no secret that I wanted to learn what he had learned from the Spokane cops. Military police tactics were old and out-of-date; we all knew that. Talking to Suggs was like jumping ahead twenty years in tactics and techniques, compared to the mindset that we were taught as military police, or MPs. Suggs started to mentor me when he realized that I really was interested in the newer, cutting-edge tactics being taught on the streets of Spokane.

He tested the waters with me one night to see how committed I was to learning the newer stuff. He called for a meeting over the handheld radio, and I met him in a parking lot. He had another cop meet us there as well. The other guy was newer, like me, and Suggs had been working with him, too—teaching him, undoing the mindset the military had instilled in him.

Suggs asked me how comfortable I was with the military's standard search technique. Did I think that I could find a gun or knife and still keep my suspect under control? Yeah, I did. I was pretty physically fit and cocky. I thought there was no way a suspect could get the best of me, search or not. I worked out constantly; it was a life-long obsession. I told him I was pretty good at searching. He smiled, and I knew I had just made a mistake.

He laid out the scenario for me. A guy had broken through the gates of the installation, and was trying to access the nuclear-loaded aircraft area. I had stopped him and removed him from his vehicle and now had to search him. Suggs cut out the normally tedious and long-winded process of removing the suspect from the vehicle, which is similar to the current "felony stop" procedures police now use and took me straight to the search. This was to be a test of my toughness and my real desire to learn, as I was about to find out.

He had me start to search the "suspect"—the other cop, a guy I didn't know—and as soon as I found the weapon, everything went to shit. Suggs had told this guy to fight like his life depended on it as soon as I found the weapon.

The fight was on. This was not like the military training I had been accustomed to. This guy turned on me and was seriously kicking my ass. There was no time out. It was a no-holds-barred, fifteen-minute dog fight. By the end of the fight, we were both bloodied up pretty good. Uniforms were torn, and our usually highly polished boots were shredded. Neither one of us could defeat the other.

The idea of searching and containing the suspect was gone. I was raging mad, and so was the "suspect." Suggs watched us fight and was talking shit to me the entire time, telling me I was losing and that I was going to die. He said, "I thought you wanted to be a cop? This is a sad excuse for police work—you've let your suspect kick your ass." He kept talking shit to me until I was finally able to get the guy into an arm-bar and nearly broke his arm. I was taunting him by this point, yelling, "Now what? Now what?"

Then Suggs stopped the fight. He separated us, standing between us, keeping us at arm's length. For us, the fight was not over. This had gone 'way beyond training. Suggs laughed at us and told the other guy to go to his car. He left, staring at me the entire time. "Mad dogging," we would later call it on the street.

Suggs said to me, "Okay. I see that you're serious and want to learn. First thing that you need to learn is you can never take for granted that you are gonna make it home. You survive the night by being meaner, tougher and, most importantly, smarter than the other guy. You get cocky like you were tonight and you're gonna get killed."

He said that was the most important thing he learned from Spokane's cops. He said they did the same thing to him. They had him search a "suspect" and then it went to shit. He had to fight until he too overcame his "suspect." They told him 75 percent of the cops who came to their academy failed this test and were washed out.

"Congratulations," he said to me. "You just passed their first test."

Over the next several months we had a number of meetings like this one. They weren't as violent, but they were just as challenging. Suggs always had a concept to teach, or an idea or technique that I had to learn, practice, and master. He taught me a lot. The most important thing he taught me was always to challenge what I was being taught. To make it work for me on the streets or get rid of it. He changed my mentality from following the rules and conforming to the ways that the military had taught me to what actually carried me through my entire career. Challenge everything: every technique, every theory, and every tactic. Right or wrong, he shaped the way I saw police work from then on.

Several months later, Suggs was slated to get out of the military. His enlistment was up. I thought he'd surely be picked up by the Spokane PD. He told me as he left that he had tested for the police department and had scored well, ranking #1 on their list. He was confident he'd be hired. I never learned what happened after that. Later on, I heard that they did not pick him up and that he had failed the psychological exam—but that was a rumor, and I never knew for sure. It was certainly hard for me to believe.

As an MP, he was head and shoulders above the rest of us. He was an expert marksman, fit, and took the job to another level. He was very professional in the way he dressed and acted. He studied regulations and laws, and, as I said, he worked as a reserve for the Spokane PD.

Fast forward: several years have passed, and I too have left the military police corps. I'm working for the sheriff's department back home in St. Paul's. I was fortunate to be picked up by the sheriff's department at a time when hundreds of people would test for only one or two job openings.

One night I was writing a report on an aggravated assault I'd been investigating. The tempers of patrons at a local truck stop had erupted into a knife fight. Two men were fighting over a woman: one was her husband, the other, her boyfriend. The husband stabbed the boyfriend and the woman called the cops. We investigated the incident, and I'd returned to the office to write my report.

I was sitting at a table we all used to write reports. We wrote them by hand then. PCs were a couple of years away from being practical. I took a break from writing, stretching my hands and looking around the room at the wanted posters hanging on the wall. Suggs had taught me well, and I always kept up on the latest twix, teletypes, and wanted photos available. The other deputies called me paranoid—not for the first or last time in my career.

One of the posters caught my eye. The guy looked really familiar. He was wanted by the FBI. I looked at him and tried to place him in my memory....I couldn't remember where I had last seen him. The name listed the wanted man as Robert Michael Allen. The name did not ring any bells, but then, as now, I never forget a face. The face for me is a lock; once I know your face I'll never forget you. I can't remember names as easily.

At first, I was puzzled. I knew this face, but from where? The name was totally unfamiliar to me. I read the poster, and it said that Allen had murdered a movie producer and the producer's father and son. They'd been involved in a business deal and had stolen a couple of hundred thousand dollars from Allen. When Allen discovered the theft he was furious and killed them, shooting them all. The wanted poster listed Allen as a "bodyguard" by profession, who was an expert marksman and an avid gambler. He was considered armed and very dangerous.

I kept looking at the face. Somewhere I knew I had met this guy. At first I accused the other guys in the office of playing a prank on me by making up a fake wanted poster and using a picture of someone I knew as the bad guy. It made sense; we were always playing pranks on each other to break up the tension we all felt. They all looked at me like I was crazy. The Sergeant told me to "quit being an attention whore and get back to your report." I ignored him. I knew that I knew this face.

The poster detailed a few facts about Allen—his height and weight, eye color, scars. He had a bullet wound on the big toe of one foot, and several aliases. Reading the aliases, I was stunned. While Robert Michael Allen was his given legal name, one of his aliases was Robert Michael Suggs.

The light finally came on in my head. The FBI now wanted the same "Suggs" who had mentored me years earlier in the military for a triple homicide in Culver City, California. He was on the run, armed, and dangerous.

I pulled the poster off of the wall and said, "Holy shit, I know this guy!"

The sergeant replied, "Yeah, yeah—sure you do. We all know someone wanted by the FBI."

"No, really—I know this guy, I was in the military with him. He was a cop then and mentored me."

"That explains a lot!" the sergeant replied. "You were mentored by a murderer. Lemme see the fucking poster."

I handed it to him. "It says here to call the FBI if you have any information about him. Maybe you should call them, Deputy."

He smirked and looked at the other deputies in the room, and they all started laughing. They thought I was full of shit. I watched this room full of rednecks laughing and giggling about how they were making a fool out of the city boy. None of them had ever left the county they were born in. None had ever worked a murder, or knew a murderer. I had grown up in the city. I saw my first murder at six years of age. It happened across the street from our house. I had known several of the local hardcore criminals in my neighborhood from the time we were all little kids and growing up on the same streets. This bugged the hell out of my co-workers.

I thought it over and said "Yeah, you're right, I should call. Can I use the phone on your desk?"

The room went silent.

"Sure, go ahead, knock yourself out," the sergeant said.

I picked up the phone and started to dial the number. The sergeant suddenly took the receiver from me and hung up the phone glaring at me. He redialed the number from the poster and handed me the receiver. This was unreal.

The FBI answered the phone, and I told them what I knew about Suggs. The agent I spoke to was condescending as hell and said that Suggs was a killer and that they would find him. I told them he was well-trained and had been a reserve officer with the Spokane police. That information was not on the wanted poster, and the FBI guy suddenly took me seriously. He asked my name, and spent the next forty-five minutes picking my brain about Suggs.

He then asked where I worked and if he could reach me if anything came up. I said sure. The room was still silent. The sergeant who was so sarcastic was now silent and blankly staring at me. It was a snapshot of what my entire career would be like. An outsider, walking the line between cops and killers, fitting in with neither.

I kept track of Suggs from that point on. About a year later I learned that his body and that of his girlfriend had been found in the California desert. Apparently his girlfriend had been trying to break up with him at the same time that he had been ripped off by the movie producer. Suggs kidnapped her and later killed her. I made a point of telling my arrogant sergeant about Suggs's fourth murder and his apparent suicide. He had no comment.

This story is an excellent example of what later became a very common and amazing scenario with the cops I worked with and around. I call it Hero-to-Zero Syndrome.

Every one of the cops listed in this book was outstanding in his or her own way. Every single one went from being considered an exceptional cop, respected by his peers, to being a criminal, publically humiliated—or at the very least no longer a cop. All were handed their walking papers and asked not to return. If there is any common denominator among them, it is that they identified strongly with being a cop.

You can read about Suggs on the web. Google the name Robert Michael Allen. He is listed as #434 on the FBI's Most Wanted list. He was a good cop when I knew him, and he was also, later, a multiple murderer.

He is the only cop I will list by his real name here. The rest of the stories related here are also true, but the names of the people involved have been changed. The cops were real cops, each outstanding in his or her own way. Somehow, they all went down in flames.

CHAPTER TWO

JAMES TUCKER

JAMES TUCKER JOINED THE POLICE department in St.Pauls after serving on a mission for his church. He was a poster boy for wholesome goodness. He never drank alcohol, he never swore at anyone. He'd have an absolute shit fit if you used the words "Jesus" or "God" in anything but a prayer. I have no idea what the hell he was doing as a cop.

I first met him on a call after he was finished probation and out on the street on his own. He was very straitlaced, wound so tight and so perfect. He had significant trouble speaking to the people we dealt with on the street. I literally had to translate for him when we were on calls together. Here is a brief example of the conversations we had:

> Tucker: Sir, I am Officer Tucker. This is Officer Fortier. I am responding to your request for police assistance.
>
> Dude: What?
>
> Me: He wants to know what happened, why you called the cops.
>
> Dude: Oh, yeah! Well, my fucking neighbor's dog keeps shitting on my lawn. I told the motherfucker I was gonna kill his fucking dog if it happened again and he said that he would kill me if I killed his fucking dog. I want the goddamn dog to stop shitting on my lawn.
>
> Tucker: Sir, I may be of assistance; however, you must please stop using the Lord's name in vain.

Dude: HUH?

Me: He's gonna help you, but watch your fucking mouth. (Tucker grimaced)

Dude: Oh, Okay. Sorry.

The rest of the call went like that. It was weird to work with a cop this squeaky-clean. He never swore. He was stiff as a board and walked like he had a stick up his ass. He was really out of his element on the streets, but he had wanted to be a cop his whole life and nothing was gonna change that.

We continued to work the same areas but on different shifts, rarely overlapping on calls. Once in a while he'd show up on a call and listen to me. He pulled me aside once and asked me "How did you learn to talk like them?"

"What?"

"I've seen you talk to different people from all walks of life; it's like you switch vocabularies when you speak to street people."

"Yeah, well…they have a different set of rules, a totally different reality from the bank president or the college professor. I try to relate to them in their language, their comfort zone."

He said he felt like they were all trash and "less" than the upper-class people in the city. I told him that was too bad because they made our jobs possible. He asked what I meant.

"You will never get a college professor talking to you late at night in a dark parking lot about a murder he knows something about, or telling you about a drug dealer he knew. These are the people who help us make arrests. All they want is a little respect. You give them that and they'll remember it." He seemed to think about this, but made no comment.

Tucker continued in his structured, black-and-white thinking. One of the brass in our department was watching him and began to mentor him. He convinced Tucker that he was too good for the streets. This mentor told him that he needed to go back to school and finish his degree. He suggested that Tucker maybe get a job with the Drug Enforcement Administration (DEA) or the Bureau of Alcohol,

Tobacco and Firearms (ATF). Tucker liked this idea. He started back
to school when he wasn't at work.

I didn't work with him much after that. We would pass occasionally in the report-writing room, or in court. I remember once he was
booking a suspect into jail for possessing drug paraphernalia. I asked
him what he had. "Scales, needles, a kit?" On the street, a kit was called
"the works." It was everything you needed to shoot up: needle, spoon,
cotton to filter the drug with when you draw it into the syringe, a
lighter, and a piece of rubber tubing to wrap around your arm to make
the veins stand out.

Tucker said the guy had a pipe. He showed me a short, hand-held
pot pipe. It held one hit.

I said "Really? That's it?"

"Yes. It's a class "B" violation. He's going to jail."

I shook my head. He looked at me disapprovingly.

He said, "I'm not like you. You're jaded. I enforce all the laws equally.
If you break the law, I will arrest you."

I said, "Okay, Cagney. Where's Lacey?"

He glared at me.

I said, "'Sup to you, man, but I say step on the pipe and make sure
the guy knows he owes you one. Maybe you quit making misdemeanor
arrests and start making felony arrests? Just a thought."

He glared at me and continued on with the booking sheet.

Much later, I ran into him in court. He was mad as hell, so I asked,
"What's wrong, Tucker?"

"I can't believe it!" He was fuming.

"What?"

Tucker snarled, "I'd arrested a guy for assault and having a concealed
weapon. The guy had a knife on him, and when I arrested him I found
it in the frisk search. I measured the closed pocketknife, and it was a
half-inch longer than the law allowed. I added the charge of a dangerous concealed weapon to the other charges. When I arrived at court, the
prosecutor had thrown out the concealed dangerous weapon charge!"

Tucker was pissed. He'd personally measured the knife, and it was
too long. He told the prosecutor this and the prosecutor just shrugged

and said, "The charges are dropped; they were ridiculous." The black-and-white Tucker was furious.

I just said, "Sorry man." Reality sometimes hurt like that for guys like Tucker.

I heard later on that he was dating one of the dispatchers. She'd made a point out of letting everyone know that she was interested in him. She pursued him like a lioness stalking her prey.

Every Samson has his Delilah.

He never knew what hit him. He was out of his element on the streets, but here with this lioness, he was truly prey. He was in deep shit. She reeled him in like a pro.

They were married soon after, following all the rules of his chosen religion, jumping through all the hoops, making everything legit. Tucker would have it no other way. He was that kind of guy, by the book, to the letter, every "T" crossed, every "I" dotted. His perfect life was intact. He married his perfect bride and continued in school.

The next time I saw Tucker, I'd already heard he was leaving the police department. He had an impeccable resume, and had applied to one of the government agencies with the three-letter acronyms. FBI, CIA, ATF, DEA, CIA—you get the picture. He was on his way off of the street and into the big time.

He was strutting around that last day I saw him, proud, as he should have been. His life was a movie poster, picture-perfect. He followed the rules, he went to church, and he never drank, smoked, or swore. He'd married the perfect girl. He was a "blue flamer," on the fast track to success. Big blue flames were virtually shooting out of his ass on his way to the top. Big things were in store for him.

Tucker successfully graduated from the required federal law-enforcement academies, and was transferred to a neighboring state, to begin his federal law-enforcement career. He had all his ducks in a row, like usual.

The lieutenant who had mentored him bragged about his protégé, telling us that Tucker's success was due in large part to the lieutenant's influence and guidance. He continually updated us on Tucker's success stories. He was living vicariously through Tucker's success, I suppose. He got on my fucking nerves.

About a year later, I heard that Tucker was back in our state. He'd requested a transfer because his wife had a potentially fatal disease that could only be treated at a special medical facility that was located in our state. The agency he worked for had granted the transfer immediately. I really felt bad for the dude. This shit was heartbreaking. He had toed the line his whole life, and now his wife was really sick and might not survive.

My own life, meanwhile, was a constant train wreck, with divorce after divorce. I hated any authority figure, and I rarely did what I was supposed to. It was odd as hell how things worked out. I felt sick for him.

Tucker did what any man should do: he stood by his wife, supporting her. He was a rock. She was dying, and he showed nothing but kindness and support for her. I was extremely impressed. I could see the end of this saga: he'd stay at her side, doing whatever he could to make her comfortable. He would never leave her in this condition. It was not in him. He would not quit. He did not know how to quit. He would not leave her no matter what. For him, marriage was for eternity. Literally.

Time passed, and the family held fundraisers to help pay for the expensive treatments Tucker's wife needed. The community reached out to them as well, and donations were made to a bank account; thousands of dollars were raised to pay for the cutting-edge medical tests and treatments that she required.

His mentoring lieutenant let us know how we could all donate to help pay for his wife's care. Meanwhile, Tucker's wife herself held up remarkably well. She hardly looked sick at all, and people remarked at her strength, and will to live. She was as strong and determined as he was to see this through. They were both inspiring people.

Then one day, a family member became suspicious. Tucker's sick wife never looked sick, and she never received the treatments that were scheduled. Every time an appointment would be made for treatment, something would come up, and the treatment would be cancelled. The suspicious relative started to pry, and eventually the "dying wife" came clean.

She told the observant family member that she and Tucker had fabricated the story about her illness to manipulate Tucker's employer into transferring them back to her hometown to be near her mother. She missed her mom, and she claimed Tucker knew all about the ruse from the beginning. They had fabricated a letter from a fictional doctor outlining her illness. There was no illness, ever.

The family member turned them both in for fraud.

Tucker's wife ended up cutting a deal with the prosecutors and testifying against him. She claimed it was his idea to move, and that he had suggested the plan they followed. She helped fabricate the documents they'd used to dupe the agency he worked for into transferring him, but she claimed it was all his idea.

Tucker ended up losing everything. His career was over. He was a convicted felon several times over when she was done testifying against him. He was disgraced in the law-enforcement community and humiliated on the evening news.

I thought back on the squeaky-clean Tucker I knew on the streets and wondered if there were any way he could've done this. I don't think there was. I think she lied to him and made everything up until he was in too deep to save the situation.

Tucker had one major flaw. He was loyal to a fault. He was raised to believe that the person you married was sent to you by God himself. You were preordained in heaven to marry this person. That was what he had been taught from the time he was a child. To abandon his wife, to turn her in for fraud, would have been an act against his God and meant that his entire life was a sham. He couldn't do, accept, or believe that, and I think it destroyed him.

CHAPTER THREE
RAY (ARNOLD) FOSSUM

RAY FOSSUM WAS TRULY AN amazing cop. He had an incredible knack for the streets. I first met him when we were both testing for different job openings at the various police departments in the area where I lived.

We would pass each other in the testing rooms, doing the head nod that guys do in silent acknowledgement, no words passed. Then if we both passed the test, we would compete in the PT tests. He could do more push-ups, and I could run faster. We competed against each other but also encouraged each other. Friendly rivals, competitors, each wanting the same thing.

In a few years we were both working for the same police department; he was hired about a year before I was. We had actually grown up on different sides of the same city, and we ended up working for the city's PD. We both liked working nights, and ended up on opposing night shifts.

He was a constantly moving mass of nervous energy. One leg was always bouncing. He was always talking. When he laughed it was always a nervous, edgy, loud laugh. Watching him, I always wondered what made him tick.

I was raised in the central part of the city. He was raised on the east side by affluent parents. His dad was a professor at the local college; mine was a mechanic. We each had our reasons for wanting to be a cop in the city we'd grown up in. We each had our demons.

Ray had a picture-perfect career. He started in patrol working nights, like I did. He'd been working for about a year when he was selected for the most recent political hot potato: the Gang Task Force.

The gang problem was out of control in the city, and the new chief needed to at least appear to have taken some kind of action. Ray and two other guys were selected to augment the task force in a high-profile move to appease the city council and the media. They were given the impossible task of turning the gang problem around immediately.

They were in the paper almost nightly—press releases, news articles. Ray was right in the middle of it. He was making a difference, and attracting women like moths to a flame—two things that Ray excelled at.

One night Ray was sent to respond to a report of a drunken patron of a strip bar in the north end of the city. Most guys would have arrived, picked the guy up, and then taken him to jail for the quick slam dunk and get back on the streets.

Ray arrived and, as usual, he started to dig. He later told me that he just looked at the guy and he knew that something was wrong with him. He said the guy "felt all wrong." Ray kept at it, digging, verifying information, and checking on small details that the guy told him about—where he had been and who he was. His identification was not in the databases, his social security did not match his name—things about him just looked wrong.

Ray had a sixth sense for this shit, and he was almost never wrong. He eventually discovered that the bald, nerdy, middle-aged and overweight drunk who had been getting loud and obnoxious at the strip club was wanted for multiple counts of rape in several neighboring states.

He was a serial rapist who would set up appointments with female real estate agents and then get them alone in vacant homes, rape them, tie them up, and then leave. He had been on the run for several years and was very successful at not getting caught.

Until he ran into Ray. Ray ended that cocksucker's free ride in a few short minutes while giving a clinic on what it means to be an outstanding cop.

Ray bounced from one great assignment to another. He was the go-to guy for the brass. If they had a problem Ray was an easy, obvious choice. He was photogenic, politically correct (in public), and a mass of moving energy that could not be stopped.

He bounced from one special assignment to another. Anything that required total dedication and boundless energy Ray was plugged into until the next quick fix was needed, and then he was moved to the new problem. He was a rising star in the police department, surely headed to at least the rank of lieutenant—possibly assistant chief.

Watching Ray, though, you could see he had something deep and dark inside that haunted him. Like I said, he was constantly in motion.

I remember stopping to talk to him and one of the senior officers in a parking lot one slow night. The older guy was calm, seasoned. He was watching us both like a father watches his sons: seeing everything through the filter of experience, making very few comments, but always listening.

It was never more obvious to me than that night just how wound up Ray was. He was sitting in the driver's seat of the patrol car. The car was stationary; Ray was not. He never stopped moving the entire time. He looked like a meth addict, constantly moving—twitching, leg bouncing, laughing too loud, talking too fast.

It really struck me then the amount of nervous energy that Ray constantly burned off. Obviously, something very deep bothered him a lot. Something he could barely contain.

Ray had one true passion aside from women. He loved sports. Any and all sports. He could talk sports, any sport, with the most rabid fan. He could talk at length about the most obscure stats of almost any player in almost any sport. I was amazed and mystified at what he found time to study and obsess over. He was a mystery to me.

I was working one of many part-time jobs in a department store when I ran into a girl who dated a friend of Ray's. She started to tell me about their double dates. She said Ray had a different girl with him every single night and "lived fast."

I said, "Yeah, Ray is the golden boy of the department."

"Yeah…I guess if they knew what I knew, he'd be fired in a second!"

I stopped cold. There was something in her voice and eyes that told me she knew something about that deep, dark secret that Ray kept so tightly under wraps.

On the outside I appeared casual, but made a mental note. I started to listen to her very carefully. I wanted to know what she knew, and I knew it would only be a matter of time and earning her trust, and then she would spill it

Several months went by, and the woman split from Ray's running buddy. She was heartbroken. Ray's friend had left his wife and moved in with her, they had rented an apartment together, set up house and home. Then she came home from work one day to find that he had left her and moved back in with his wife.

Simple as that, he left her with a lease she could not afford, bills she could not pay. She was devastated. I listened as she poured out the last few months of their relationship: dates, drinking, parties.

She got really quiet and said, "Do you remember that day I mentioned to you about Ray and his secret?"

I was instantly on alert. I remembered, but I didn't act like I was interested. I said, "Ray and his secret? No, not really."

She laid it all out. When she was done, it all made sense. The details fit into what I already knew.

Ray had been transferred to the narcotics strike force after his latest success in the department's specialty units. He had been an instant success, as was usual for Ray. He still had the boundless energy, the attention to detail, the single-minded focus on the job. He immediately started to make an impact. Ray had an intuition for narcotics, a sixth sense that was uncanny.

Ray loved to run to keep in shape, and his running partner was the sergeant of the unit—another fast-tracked, guaranteed performer who succeeded at every assignment he was given. Sergeant Billy Webster was a force to be reckoned with on the street. (He gets his own story later in this book.) The two cops were partners on and off the streets. They fit. They worked tirelessly and partied hard.

Billy Webster was the heartbroken girl's short-lived roommate/romance. She told me that both men bragged to her often about taking narcotics—pain pills, mostly—that were seized in raids while working their cases in the undercover world of the narcotics strike force.

Both of them admitted this to her as they partied at her apartment, drinking hard liquor and popping the prescription pain pills.

Each of them bragged about how they manipulated the paperwork and evidence documents during raids to hide their activities. According to her, they also bragged about how they spent money intended for undercover buys on their personal expenses, and she claimed that she had personally witnessed them popping handfuls of pain pills "like they were candy." She said that they were both barely affected by the handfuls of pills, and in her opinion they were both hard-core addicts.

I listened and thought about the suspicions I'd had for years. I have mentioned in my other books the fact that leaks would occur in the department's databases; information about informants would somehow seep out. The narcotics strike force would be planning to make a raid on a drug dealer, and ten minutes before they arrived, the phone would ring, the house would clear out, and the drugs would disappear. When they got there, there would be nothing. It all suddenly became really clear.

I listened as she recalled the conversations. It all fit; another piece of the fucked-up puzzle of the streets fell into place. This was the reality of the streets I worked, and the people I worked with.

Ray kept this demon at bay for some time. He hid in the world of undercover drug buys, fast money, and fast women. Eventually his body's tolerance for the painkillers rose to such a level that he couldn't hide the huge amounts he was stealing from the strike force's drug seizures. He needed thirty to forty pills of hard-core prescription narcotics just to make it through the day. He was a junkie.

This explained the limitless energy Ray had. He was "jonesin'." He was in withdrawal. I think that was why his leg bounced, why he kept moving and could not stop. He was in pain.

Ray's addiction eventually drove him to make a serious error. One day he was at a local pharmacy, picking up a list of people who used the place to fill their prescriptions. He cross-referenced the list against other pharmacies' lists of customers. Drug addicts who abuse prescription drugs often "doctor shop," getting multiple prescriptions and then filling them at different pharmacies. The lists were provided to law enforcement to help battle the problem.

Ray had worked himself into the prescription drug specialist for the narcotics unit. It fit his needs. He now was a wolf in charge of watching the sheep. He thought he could keep his addiction problem hidden forever. It had worked so far, so why not?

He fucked up, though.

While the pharmacist was printing the lists, Ray grabbed a couple of bottles of strong pain pills off of the shelves to feed his increasing addiction. The pharmacist had been suspicious of some earlier losses of pills and had installed hidden cameras. He knew that someone was stealing from him, he just didn't know who or how.

Ray was caught red-handed. The pharmacist reported the theft immediately. Ray ended up losing everything. His career, retirement, respect—all gone.

The people we worked with were surprised, shocked. They could not believe that Ray had done the theft. I met with Billy Webster's ex-girlfriend later and she said, "I told you they were both dropping pain pills like they were candy."

She was right. Everything she told me had been true. Webster would go down in flames as well a few months later, but for a different and unrelated incident.

CHAPTER FOUR
BILLY WEBSTER

AS AMAZING AS RAY FOSSUM was as a cop, Billy Webster was even more so. I met him one day after he had just been assigned his first tour on the narcotics strike force. I was riding as an observer with a cop I knew, trying to see if I wanted to transition from the Military Police Corps to the civilian side of the house. Billy was friends with the cop I was riding with.

We were leaving the jail after he finished booking a suspect and were crossing the parking lot, when Webster pulled up in an unmarked car. Smiling his million-dollar smile, he started laughing, making us jump to the side as he pulled up fast, stopping hard, tires screeching. I was instantly pissed off, having no idea who this metrosexual-looking crazy man was who was trying to run us over.

He said, "Hey, what's up?" to the cop I was with. I was glaring at him as they talked, and he said to the cop, "What's this guy's fucking problem?" Then to me, "Hey, we got a fucking problem here?" I didn't answer.

The other cop explained I was a ride-along, and then he told me that Billy was an undercover cop. We continued to stare at each other. I was, as I still am, stubborn as hell, and when I get mad, I'm even more so. Finally I walked away, heading back to the patrol car while the two friends talked.

Later, the cop I was riding with explained that Billy was the single most amazing cop he had ever worked with. He said that Billy had an uncanny knack for knowing what was going on in the streets. He said that it was eerie the way Webster could locate people who were on the run or hiding from the cops, and that he'd been sent to the narcotics strike force "early," meaning he was sent ahead of the normal time frame in which a cop was considered able to contribute to the unit.

I wouldn't see Webster again for some time. Four years passed, and I ended up working for the same department as Webster and Fossum. I'd spent some time in the sheriff's department and decided it wasn't for me. I had tested at the police department while working at the sheriffs department and finally been hired. I was in training, and my training officer was introducing me to the other officers in the department.

We were leaving the jail, and there was the amazing Billy Webster. He'd just left the strike force. It was his turn to rotate out and back to patrol. Webster was fatter, straining the buttons on his old uniform shirts, and out of touch with the patrol side of the streets. Narcotics is a whole other world, and he'd specialized in it.

He had a drunk driver he was booking and was obviously nervous about what to do with the suspect. He asked my training officer if he would like to have his "new" rookie take the DUI for the experience. My trainer immediately saw through this ploy and said, "Nope. You catch it, you clean it"—meaning "You caught him, the work is yours to do."

He commented on the excess weight Webster had gained and the way his buttons were barely containing his newly acquired pot gut. They exchanged "fuck-yous" and we departed.

I would run into Webster occasionally after I completed training, as our shifts overlapped and we worked the same area. He was every bit as streetwise as I'd been told. He knew everyone on every call in the inner city, and not only did he know *them*, he knew their families and associates. He was very aware of the people around him and the non-verbal communication they exchanged.

I tried to learn as much from him as I could. I was always asking questions, trying to see what he saw, hear what he heard. It seemed I could never quite understand how he grasped so well what was going on from the smallest and most insignificant details. Every call with him was an education.

I tried to keep up with him one night as he chased down, on foot, a rapist who had just broken into a house and raped a woman. Webster arrived at the scene as the guy took off on a bicycle. Webster was already out of his car, walking the area, looking for the guy. Webster saw him and sprinted off on foot after him, quickly closing the gap and tackling the suspect, knocking him off his bike and slamming him into the ground.

It was pretty cool to see his enthusiasm. Even more amazing, I later found out that he had sprinted after the rapist piece of shit on a damaged knee. He wore a knee brace every day at work and never complained.

Webster hated to lose in court as much as he hated to lose on the streets. He had a very high record of convictions in the courts, and the judges admired his ability to close a case.

I personally had a district court judge tell me while he was signing a search warrant for me that he thought very highly of Webster. He asked me if Webster was involved in the incident I was working on, for which he was signing the warrant. I told him that he wasn't. The judge said that was unfortunate, as he liked seeing him in his court. He described Webster as "ballsy" and the best cop he had ever known—which is very high praise from a sitting district court judge.

One night I was sitting with Webster in a parking lot, parked side by side and I asked him about a narcotics case he'd lost in court. It rarely happened, and he was pissed. He told me all about it and then said, "But that's okay, in the end they got theirs."

"What do you mean?"

He laughed and made me promise not to tell. I said of course I wouldn't tell. He smiled and told me that he'd gone to the suspect's house while off duty and slashed their recently purchased tires on their jacked-up 4x4 truck. The tires were hugely oversized and very expensive. Then Webster said, "No one gets one over on me, ever." He said, "What the courts won't take care of, we will. We are cops and we keep the shitbags in line, no matter what." He then smiled and drove away.

Another incident occurred when Webster was on a call with one of his friends in the department. The other cop was training a new guy we called "Skidmark." All three were sent to a child-abuse call, and when they arrived, they found that the man had indeed sexually abused this young child.

There is a special place in every cop's heart for child abusers; it is a dark place you don't want to visit. The rules start to break down there. Anger seeps in at the inadequacies of the system, and it becomes harder and harder to follow what the rest of the world sees as the right or correct thing to do.

That night, the two veteran cops lost it, and beat the abusive suspect up a bit. Not a lot, but more than the self-righteous Skidmark could live with. He turned them in to the department's internal affairs unit. They were investigated and given time off without pay after having been found to be in the wrong on the incident.

It isn't pretty, but it happens. All cops have been there. Webster's street-cred went up with his fellow cops for caring enough about the abused child to lose it on the suspect and beat his ass. Meanwhile, Skidmark had sealed his fate on the department as a rat and a snitch.

Webster lived larger than life when off duty. Cops don't make much money, but he often went on Caribbean cruises with his wife and kids. They owned a new motor home and a new boat, and had recently purchased a new home on the southeast side of the city.

When other cops questioned him about the lifestyle he lived, he claimed his wife made a lot of money at her job, and that he was a better money manager than they were. He added that he was also in the National Guard, and made money there. Cops are a suspicious bunch, and no one bought this explanation.

One night while I was out to dinner with a couple of old-timers from the force, I heard them discuss the tight- knit group of friends Webster had and how they all lived above the standard a cop could normally afford. These guys had seen a lot in twenty-or-more years of law enforcement, and they knew that if it walked like a duck and quacked like a duck, it was probably a duck—even if you couldn't prove it. I listened and watched.

Webster had a friend who owned a towing company in the city. Often the friend would ride along when Webster worked at night, accompanying him on the calls he was assigned. Webster was known as a "shit magnet," meaning he could get into some very hairy situations, so going on calls with him was always an adrenaline rush. The two friends went on vacations together and hung out often when they were not at work. Everyone was suspicious of the friendship.

The towing company started to receive more than its share of tows from the crashes handled by the department, and the other towing companies complained. The department policy stated that there would be an automatic rotation of the towing companies selected by dispatch unless the drivers involved in a crash requested a particular company.

When drivers did select the company, more often than not, they would request the towing company that belonged to Webster's best friend. This was investigated over and over at the request of the rest of the towing companies in the city; however, nothing was ever found to be suspicious. This went on for several years.

Webster was as adept at department politics as he was on the street, and started to get promoted up the food chain—first to sergeant, and then later tested for lieutenant. He was next in line to promote. He was once again sent to the narcotics strike force, this time as the supervising sergeant.

The strike force flourished under his supervision: arrests went up, drug seizures went up. Under his tutelage, the strike force seized an unprecedented volume of vehicles used in narcotics transactions. The proceeds from the sales of those seized vehicles came back to the strike force after the courts upheld the seizures.

Webster was a rising star in the department, on his way to at least assistant chief.

That was when Webster's personal life started to go to shit. His high-maintenance wife was having an affair, and he used strike-force wiretaps to monitor her phone conversations with her boyfriend illegally from his own home. He told me about the affair one day at a local clothing store where we both worked part-time providing security.

He began dating, and later moved in with, one of the women who worked sales at a nearby cosmetics counter. After they broke up a few months later, she told me about the wiretaps he did at home and his addiction to painkillers. I did not believe her at first, but later it all fell into place.

After his second stint on the narcotics strike force, Webster came back to patrol as a sergeant. He was still dealing with a lot of personal issues, and perhaps that made it harder to keep his extracurricular activities on the down low. It became clear that he had a personal investment in making sure that his buddy's towing company received a majority of the tows from the department.

I was present when he went up to another towing company's driver and told him that he would arrest him if he did not leave an accident scene. He then convinced the driver to request his friend's company, telling the driver that they were the best in the city.

His interest was more than just looking out for a friend, that part was obvious. At the time, however, I was generally viewed as paranoid and seeing conspiracies where there were none, so I did not comment. I filed the incident away mentally as noteworthy and continued to watch.

One night I was on a call and Webster showed up. He was usually calm and cool; even during his wife's affair, very few people knew what was going on. That night, however, I could see that he was noticeably shaken.

Something had him worried, and I asked him about it. He said that I was seeing things and that I was paranoid (yeah, yeah—I heard that my whole career). I replied, "Yep, it's me, seeing things again, sure. That's why you're shitting yourself with fear."

Webster didn't respond. Another sergeant showed up and they dismissed me, basically telling me to leave while they discussed sergeant matters.

I was not about to be dismissed by anyone. I was on a call. I said, "Hey, this is *my* call—you showed up, you leave!"

Normally that would not have floated past two veteran sergeants. It was a test, and they failed. I should have had my ass kicked on the spot for being insubordinate. Instead, they shrugged and walked about fifty feet away to talk.

Later I found out, after bugging Webster about the incident, that he was being investigated. The rumors about his ties to the towing company were flying again. The other sergeant who had shown up was involved in the investigation, and Webster had asked him off the record how serious the charges were. Webster told me the other sergeant had said that they would "take care of it," and not to worry. Webster was noticeably relieved.

A week later, he was relieved of duty while the investigation blossomed. Several of Webster's friends were then also relieved of duty, and they and Webster were eventually fired. All were accused of violating the department's policy on tow trucks being called to car crashes. They were never formally charged, however; Webster was a force to be reckoned with on the streets of our city—street wise, smart, and tough.

But his career was over.

Many years later I would talk to Ray Fossum about the tow truck incident involving Webster. He said that Webster offered him an opportunity to make money by taking kickbacks of cash from his best friend's towing company in exchange for directing tows to them. He said Webster had been doing it for years, and that in exchange for the information Fossum had on Webster, the county attorney had offered to reduce Fossum's prescription drug charges.

Fossum refused to tell what he knew about his friend, and went over to Webster's home to tell him what had happened. He said that when he arrived, Webster took him into the garage and turned up a stereo as loud as it would go. While the sound was echoing off the walls, Webster said, "Go ahead, talk now!"

Fossum was devastated. Webster evidently didn't trust him, and thought that he was wearing a wire; the music would have made it impossible for any wire to pick up the conversation they had. Fossum said that he told Webster, "Fuck you, man!" and left.

They were two of the best cops I would ever meet. Each had his demons. Each went painfully down in flames.

CHAPTER FIVE
LANCE EDWARDS

WE'D HIRED A LOT OF new guys to deal with the turnover created by the hiring of a new chief. He was hell-bent on making his mark on the department's culture and getting rid of what he considered deadwood. He defined "deadwood" as anyone nearing retirement.

Personally, I think that the veterans threatened him. They knew who he really was, since he too, had risen through the ranks. They all knew his public face nowhere near matched the reality of the prick he really was. He was busy pushing them out, and replacing them with new hires.

That was when Lance Edwards came to be a patrolman in our department.

He was a former MP, and came to the department with a wealth of experience in the military police environment. He had travelled the world, enforcing military laws. He retired from the military and was immediately picked up by our department.

He loved police work—seriously loved the job and most everything about it. He immediately made a name for himself as an outstanding patrolman. He had a knack for finding stolen cars that was unprecedented. It was an amazing and quirky gift. He recovered more stolen cars than anyone else on the department, and he continued to do so the entire time he worked for us.

I asked him to teach me his technique for recovering the stolen cars one night, and he showed me dozens of lists of stolen cars he had made from BOLOs ("be on the lookout") that had been put out by dispatch.

He cross-referenced them, making lists just for Chevys, just for trucks, just for out-of-state plates, and just for four-door vehicles. When he saw a car whose description fit one of the lists and felt it was suspicious, he would look up the plate, and *boom*! There it would be.

He also had a knack for making felony arrests. He made more felony arrests than any other patrolman in the department. It was not that he made just a couple more arrests; he made a lot more arrests. He made more DUI arrests than any other patrolman in the city, and nearly as many as the entire patrol section combined. He had a knack for finding drunk drivers that was creepy; it was almost like a sixth sense.

He was a poster boy for the kind of cop the chief wanted. He would drop anything and everything to come to work and cover a shift. He would work any shift he was called to fill and complete any task he was asked to do. He really loved being a cop.

The chief was elated, and used him as an example of what the "new" patrolman should aspire to be. This was what he was looking for when he pushed out the old guard—blue flamers, go-getters, guys who could make a difference, and for a smaller paycheck than the grizzled and, in his words, "lazy veterans" he had pushed into retirement.

The chief recognized Lance Edwards as Patrolman of the Year several times. The chief bragged about his "new breed of patrolman" in chiefs' meetings, and mentioned Lance often to the city council.

Lance had a pretty amazing reputation right away. He was also very social, which is unusual for a cop. He liked to party, and would often have friends over to his house. He had a passion for camping, and his camping parties quickly gained popularity among the patrolmen. He invited everyone, and played no favorites with any of the internal social cliques in the department. Detectives and patrolmen were all invited. The parties were quietly talked about in the hallways of the department, whispered about in the weight room, mentioned in the twenty-four hour convenience stores while guys were getting a quick drink.

Rumors of wife-swapping and public sex acts on a drunken dare started to emerge from the parties as people started to open up about the goings on. Lance was an instant favorite among the more wild and reckless patrolmen.

I asked Lance about the rumors one night, and he laughed and denied that anything like that had ever happened. Later, however, when I pressed him about the rumors, he admitted that he had on several occasions been involved in sex parties, and he had, in fact, on a dare, had sex with a woman on a picnic table while his partygoers watched.

"She was willing and I was willing, so what the fuck?" He laughed about it.

I asked him if his wife was cool with it.

"Hell, no!" he said. "She wasn't there. She's never invited to the parties I have. That would defeat the whole reason for having the party in the first place."

This was his life for several years: exemplary service as a patrolman, and wild drunken parties off duty. He eventually bought a boat, and the parties were transferred to the nearby lakes and reservoirs in the area. I actually talked to one cop's wife who heard about the parties and asked her husband if she could go out on the boat with Lance. I guess her husband had no problem with the idea of his wife and Lance on the boat together, or maybe he had no idea of what happened there; I don't know. I do know Lance and the other man's wife each bragged in great detail to their friends later about the day they spent on the boat.

The chief never heard about the parties, or if he did, he didn't mention them in his bragging about the new breed of patrolman he had hired to make a difference in the city.

Finally, the lifestyle and partying caught up to Lance. He believed that his wife never had any idea of his parties and what went on at them. She was not, however, blind, and eventually got fed up.

She was devastated at first by the betrayal, but eventually found her own distractions. She had a steady boyfriend whom she would meet while Lance was camping or on the boat with the "boat babes." Lance had no idea, and when he found out, his reaction was surprising.

One day I came to work to find that Lance had left—just left. There was no explanation, no note from the chief. Lance was just gone. No one knew if he had quit or been fired. I asked around, and all I could find out was he was gone and no one knew why. It was very odd.

Usually there were rumors floating around. They were almost always wrong, and they were almost always wild and crazy stories that were nearly impossible to believe. This time, I guess, the brass decided not to assist the rumor mill.

No matter who I asked, they all shrugged and said they had no idea where Lance had gone or why. The shining example of the chief's new breed of patrolman had just disappeared. It would be several years before I would find out what happened.

Eventually, I did run into Lance when we were both working another job, and I asked him what had happened. Where had he disappeared to, and why?   He told me that he had discovered that his wife had been having an affair behind his back for years. He was really pissed off about it and could not believe that she would do that to him. He said that he had gotten really drunk and written a suicide/ homicide note explaining why he killed her and then himself.

He was waiting for her to come home, drinking the entire time. Eventually (and fortunately, as he said later), he passed out. His wife came home and found him, the note, and the loaded handgun.

She immediately called the police. Lance was charged with attempted homicide. Eventually a plea deal was reached, and his charges were dropped. But he lost his job, and the chief lost his exemplary patrolman. In the blink of an eye, Lance went from Patrolman of the Year to being unable to get a job anywhere as a cop ever again.

CHAPTER SIX

RAY ZELLER

I FIRST MET RAY ZELLER on a report of a "beer run" at a local grocery store. Late one night we received a report that a group of young men had entered one of the larger retail grocery stores on the north side of the city. They scattered when they entered the store, as was a standard tactic for shoplifters; that way, any store security could not possibly follow them all. They'd agreed to meet back up at a beer display, and each was supposed to grab a case of beer and run back to the car. Ta-da! Instant beer run! What made this beer run different was that the initial report came in saying that shots had been fired.

I arrived with several other units and began to investigate the incident. The investigation revealed that a guy who worked at the store as a stocker had realized what was happening and taken it personally.

He had recently purchased a Glock .45-caliber handgun and had kept it concealed while he worked. He said this was for his "protection." He claimed that when he realized the group was stealing from the store, he positioned himself at the only exit and confronted them.

A brief struggle broke out, but he was outnumbered five-to-one, and the teenagers were able to get past him; one dropped a case of beer, but the others did not. The stocker gave chase and claimed that the carload of beer thieves shot a single gunshot at him as they drove away.

He felt that "for his own protection" he needed to fire back with his Glock .45…several times. He squeezed off four rounds, to be exact, as the suspects drove off. We found no witnesses who saw the beer thieves shoot at the stocker. The only other person to see the incident was another stocker, and he said that no shots were fired from the car at his co-worker.

Once we were done investigating, we all huddled up and hashed over the evidence. None of us believed that the stocker had been shot at. There was no need for the thieves to shoot at him, as they had already begun to escape. We all pretty much agreed that the stocker was a nut case, trigger-happy and looking to make a name for himself. We'd decided to arrest him when the night shift lieutenant showed up and wanted to be briefed on the incident.

We briefed him and he laughed and said, "It's about time someone put the fear of God into these fucking thieves." He told us to make no arrests, and let the county attorney sort this mess out.

Most of the cops present were not happy about this. Deadly force is nothing to joke about, and definitely not called for to stop a beer run. The lieutenant made it clear that he thought this was a case of street justice, and even went over to praise the stocker for his efforts. We all rolled our eyes and got back into our cars. Several hours of paperwork were in front of us to justify the lack of police action the lieutenant demanded.

Several years later, when the beer run call was a thing of the past, I was back in patrol and working nights. I was assigned a new officer to train, as his normal training officer had called in sick.

New guys had to be with trained and certified training officers. I'd reluctantly agreed to become an FTO (field training officer) to help train some of the chief's new "super recruits" brought in to replace the old-guard veterans the chief had pushed out of the department. So the new guy showed up to ride with me and introduced himself as Ray Zeller.

He immediately rubbed me the wrong way. He knew everything there was to know, and always had a smart-ass comment for anything I tried to teach him. I'd been involved in a shooting recently, and that was all he wanted to talk about. He asked all the usual stupid questions: *What was it like? Are you upset you didn't kill the guy? Do you have any nightmares?* Jesus, this was going to be a long night.

I was beginning to wonder if the new guy had made his training officer sick of work or if the guy truly was sick. My gut feeling was that he just needed a break from this dipshit.

I made up my mind to try to make the best of the night, and started to pick the new guy's brain. I always tried to get a feeling for a trainee's life experience and what he or she brought to the job that would help out on the streets. He liked the idea that I was asking him about himself, and started to talk and talk and talk some more. I figured I would need a drink when this shift was over.

He was blabbing on and on about himself, and suddenly he said that he, too, had been involved in a shooting. I was thinking that maybe he was in a drive-by at a party, or that he was possibly a reformed gang member. (Our department had recently hired several allegedly reformed gang members. The wisdom of these hiring's I would never understand.) I asked him if he had been in a gang?

"No," he said, "I wasn't a gang member."

He then proceeded to tell me how he had stopped an armed robbery several years ago and had gotten in a shootout with the suspects. He said that he felt that his actions that night were the reason the chief had hired him.

"Oh, yeah? Really? Where did this happen?"

He began to recall …the night of the beer run shooting. Only this time, several shots were fired at him. He fired back in self-defense, and only after he had no other choice. He said the "stupid cops did nothing that night" and "it made me want to join the police force and make a difference."

I was instantly pissed off. I said, "Hey, motherfucker, I was one of those stupid cops that night, and if we had not been ordered to let you slide you would've been arrested. So tell me again how many rounds were shot at you? Was it ONE like you said that night, or several like you are claiming now?"

Silence.

"Look, we're done here. I don't know how the fuck you got hired, but you don't belong here. I was there that night, and you don't try to kill people for stealing beer, asshole! You sit there the rest of the night and keep your fucking mouth shut."

He argued that he was in the right that night and that I was prejudiced by the event. He claimed that I had not witnessed the robbery, so I didn't know what really happened. We rode the rest of the night in silence.

I recommended that Ray Zeller be let go. He shouldn't have been working as a cop with that mentality. But he was exactly what the chief was looking for—6'2", a pretty boy, and he'd do whatever the brass told him to do. There was no doubt in my mind that he was a lawsuit waiting to happen. The brass did not get rid of Zeller, however. He stayed around, and almost immediately rumors started on the streets about him—and the streets never lie. Well…almost never.

Several years passed, and Zeller became a seasoned patrolmen. His cocky attitude had blossomed into all-out dickhead. He was married to one woman and yet having a child with another, one of the dispatchers.

A friend of mine described him as having the "golden penis syndrome"—meaning that he thought his dick was a gift to every woman he met. Maybe it was; I don't care to know. There were new stories floating around almost monthly about Zeller beating up people, degrading people he stopped or arrested.

This is the kind of shit that makes cops' jobs even harder, planting seeds of hatred and mistrust among the public for law enforcement in general. But no one would ever come forward and make a formal complaint.

They'd talk on the streets, and word got around to a few of us that Zeller was out of control. But there was not much we could do without a victim who would come forward. We listened and kept an eye out, but Zeller was careful never to fuck anyone up with a witness present.

Eventually the administration did have enough of Zeller's bullshit, and they started to prepare a file on him, preparing to fire his ass. The clock was ticking for Zeller's police career. *Tick-tock, motherfucker, karma is coming, and coming hard.*

One day a few months later, Zeller was at a mall in a nearby city with his new wife/baby momma-dispatcher. They were out celebrating Valentine's Day. He was taking his wife out to profess his love for her with dinner and a night out. Zeller, as was his usual habit, was armed with his Glock .45.

He was in cop mode 24/7/365. He felt that he always had to be armed "just in case." Zeller wanted to be sure that if anything went down, he was there to lend a hand and "make a difference."

Vlad Urlich lived near the mall, and had survived the ethnic purges in his home country of Serbia. He had survived—but barely, and was deeply scarred by the violence of the ethnic cleansing he had witnessed.

He was depressed, and having difficulty acclimating to the United States. His family was concerned about him, but they didn't know what to do to ease his mental anguish. Nothing they tried was helping.

While Ray Zeller was eating dinner with his wife, Vlad entered the mall with a loaded shotgun and began picking off people one by one. He was randomly strolling through the mall, shooting and killing anyone who came within shotgun range. It was an unbelievable scenario for most people.

People were screaming and running for their lives. Zeller heard the gunshots from the restaurant, and told his wife to stay put. He was armed, and finally his time had come to make a difference. He calmly walked out into the hallway, Glock in one hand and his badge in the other. *BOOM! BOOM!* Vlad dropped another screaming victim to his death. Zeller cautiously crept up the mall walkways, looking for the shooter.

The local police had already been called and were just arriving. The local SWAT team had several members on duty, and they had their gear in their vehicles. When they arrived, they coordinated deployment, and entered ready to take down the now-confirmed killer on a rampage.

The on-duty sergeant also entered the mall to assist the SWAT team members. He met Zeller in the hallway. Their meeting was videoed by an anonymous witness. On the video, you can see Zeller calling out to the sergeant that he himself was an off-duty cop, in the hope that he wouldn't be shot.

The reality of being the guy who "makes a difference" hit Zeller hard. He was scared shitless and terrified. The sergeant asked Zeller where the shooter was; Zeller cried out in a whining tone, "I don't know, I don't know!"

The sergeant rolled his eyes, turned his back on Zeller, and headed towards an open common area of the mall. He assumed that Zeller was following and had his back in case he got attacked from behind. The video recorded this, and then *BOOM!* Vlad had just shot another victim. The video clearly showed Ray turning and running from the scene of the shooting.

Just like that, "Billy bad ass" turned tail and ran, leaving the sergeant and the rest of the people in the mall to fend for themselves. His time to be tested had come; his true colors were shown on the video as he ran *from* the shooting and killing, while the sergeant ran *towards* it.

The next day, Zeller made national news as the "hero cop" who stopped the mall massacre. He claimed that he was there and acted to "save his buddies." The media eats this shit up. Rarely do they have this kind of cooperation from a cop who has been involved in a shooting.

Ray Zeller was present at several press conferences in full uniform, with his baby-momma wife present. The chief was also standing next to him, basking in the limelight as well. For the media, this kind of thing is a wet dream come true.

Zeller was photogenic, outgoing, talkative, gregarious, and really liked the attention they were giving him. Most cops hate the media, really dislike attention, and severely mistrust reporters, but not Zeller. He recounted a bullshit story that omitted any real detail about what he did to stop the shooter. When he was asked point-blank what he did to stop the shooting, he replied that he "did what any cop would do, he helped his buddies."

The media ate this up. Zeller made the TV talk-show circuit, appearing on Good Morning America and Larry King Live to tell lies about his heroism.

The reality is that the video shows him running away, but the mainstream media turned a blind eye to this fact. They had their good-looking poster-boy hero cop, and he liked the attention, answering any question they asked.

The chief was also happy. He finally had the perfect example of what his new breed of "super patrolman" should act and be like. He praised Zeller as one of his "finest officers," and told the press that Zeller was someone on whom he had always been able to count. The file he had been building in an attempt to fire Ray Zeller disappeared.

Meanwhile, the sergeant involved in the shooting, and the SWAT team members, were silent. There was a very real reason for this.

After any cop shoots someone, even in a case in which he shoots someone who is killing random innocent people, the cop is investigated. Every action is carefully examined. He has to have acted in accordance not only with the laws of the state and federal governments, but also with department policy. If there is any violation of any of those three things, the cop is in serious trouble.

It takes several days to sort out evidence and witness statements, and make that decision. That is why cops never comment after a shooting. They are being criminally investigated, and must be cleared before they can make any statement. Every cop knows this.

Ray Zeller knew this, and our chief knew this too. The fact that Zeller could talk the very next day after the shooting, less than 12 hours after the incident, was a silent testimony to the fact that he did nothing at all to protect anyone. Zeller didn't care though, and neither did the chief. They were two peas in a pod, both searching for recognition for their "obvious" talents. Finally they both were given their due.

The sergeant and the SWAT team members were eventually cleared of any wrongdoing after a long and intense investigation. They made an appearance on the evening news and were quickly swept under the rug. The media was not interested in the truth. They had their hero and didn't want to admit that they had been duped by Ray Zeller and his arrogant, self- serving chief.

Karma is a bitch with a long memory, and she had been looking for Ray Zeller for a long time. Zeller and the chief would soon have their payback coming. Zeller's aggressive and disrespectful ways of treating people on the street were catching up with him.

Finally a woman came forward and filed a complaint against Ray. She was drunk, loud, and abusive during a DUI stop, so Ray pulled her pants down around her ankles after he arrested her. This was typical of the stupid shit I had heard about him.

The complaint made the news, and then more people came forward to complain. The chief stood by his "super patrolman" and tried to brush off complaints against him as attempts by the public to discredit Zeller, claiming Zeller was a target of jealousy because of his heroism. The chief was still careful though, never to appear at press conferences on the subject. He always made sure an assistant chief or public affairs officer presented any press release that supported Zeller.

Then came the straw that broke the camel's back. Before he achieved hero status by running away during the mall shooting, Zeller had been on a call one night breaking up a loud party. He told the partygoers to keep the noise down, and while he was looking around, he saw a girl he liked. He came back later and convinced her to give him a blowjob while others at the party watched.

She was willing at the time; problem was, she was underage. A minor.

When she came forward with witnesses to the event, Zeller tried to deny it had ever happened. The chief again sent his spokesman to support Zeller and claim it was all lies, and that there were people out to discredit Zeller because he was a proven national hero.

It was all smoke and mirrors, of course, and Zeller was history. The chief eventually disowned him. Zeller was decertified and stripped of his police officer status, and eventually ended up in jail.

He was never a "real" hero, but he definitely hit zero. I am sure the sergeant and the SWAT team members who really did stop the killer that day had smiles on their faces at the news of Zeller's very public demise. I know I did.

CHAPTER SEVEN
ED MASCARENAS

MORE THAN ANYTHING, ED MASCARENAS wanted to be a cop. He had entered the Marines after high school and did a four-year enlistment. He did some time in Bosnia while he was in the Marines, and then elected to get out when his enlistment was up.

He applied at the police department in my city and was picked up as a non-sworn community-service officer, tasked with handling cold calls not considered important enough for sworn officers. Mascarenas immediately made a name for himself as a go-to-guy in the community service officer (CSO) group.

He came in early, stayed late, and was always available for overtime shifts. That was what the brass looked for in the new guys—workers who were willing and able to put the job above all else, make the job their only reason for living. It was a philosophy that came back to haunt them time and time again.

Police work is taxing, and even the most resilient cops get jaded and twisted from the job. The brass didn't care. They wanted production and enthusiasm. When the new guys burned out and fell apart, they'd just get more young, fresh meat. This kept budget costs down and production up. Ed Mascarenas wrote more reports and handled more cold calls than any other CSO in the department. One night after he had come to patrol, I asked him how he did it, and he admitted that he took paperwork home and did cases on his off-duty time to stay ahead of the rest of the group.

"That's crazy!"

"I was going to get to sworn status no matter what it costs me, and I have to prove myself. I wouldn't let anything get in the way of my goal of being a patrolman."

It took about a year, and the brass liked what they saw: another go-getter to add to the growing list of new guys. They offered him a job on the road, and he jumped at the opportunity.

While Ed was working as a non-sworn officer, he had to do a lot of tasks in the records division—filing papers, writing cold reports, and answering the phones. He hated the work, but there was one major benefit to the job. The department had recently hired several young women as records clerks. Ed was able to spend a lot of time with the new hires, and eventually he fell hard for a nineteen-year-old clerk.

He was twenty-six, and in a dying marriage with his high school sweetheart. They had grown in totally opposite directions since Ed had decided to become a cop, and he was miserable. It took him about a nanosecond to decide that he wanted out of the marriage when he met "Victory," the nineteen-year-old records clerk.

Ed ended his marriage and became a sworn officer at about the same time. His life was turning around and his dreams were coming true. He was now a patrolman with a beautiful young girlfriend.

He started in patrol with the same enthusiasm that he had shown as a CSO. He was coming in early, going home late, and always working overtime. He appeared to be headed for greatness in the department.

He received his first medal about a year later for saving an infant who was drowning in a swimming pool in the backyard of the child's home. The child's mother had left the infant in a wading pool and had gone inside their house. She came back to find the child face-down in the pool. She called 911, but was so distraught she could not determine whether the child was breathing or not.

Ed was working that night and monitoring the dispatchers on the medical channel with his own personal police scanner. He heard the call come in about a possible drowning, and jumped the call. He arrived several minutes ahead of paramedics and started infant CPR on the drowned child. By the time paramedics arrived, he had the child breathing and crying loudly.

He was credited with saving the child, and received the department's lifesaving medal. No one could remember the last time a lifesaving medal had been awarded. Ed was proud, as he should have been. His enthusiasm and zest for the job had saved the child's life. He liked how it felt to be recognized by the chief as a hero. The local paper ran an article about him as well. He received a lot of recognition in the community for the incident.

His new girlfriend was proud as well. She beamed as she stood at his side while he was given the medal at the annual awards ceremony.

Ed doubled his efforts, made even more arrests, and handled more cases than any other officer on his squad. He fell back on the tactic of taking home cases that were not high-priority and writing them up in his off time. This enabled him to get back on the road, available sooner for the next call that came up in his area.

The brass loved it. His stats were so far above any one of the other officers' stats on his shift that they were almost double the next-highest producing officers. The sergeant praised him daily. The chief left him personal notes in his mailbox, praising his performance. The sky appeared to be the limit for him in the department.

The practice of taking paperwork home, however, eventually came back to bite Ed in the ass. He started to lose cases and case notes. The reports went unwritten, incidents were not recorded, and Ed was in trouble. He had to admit to the brass that he had been taking work home and doing it off-duty, which wasn't technically allowed. Instead of punishing him though, they gave him a slap on the wrist and sent him back out on the street. He was told to keep up his strong work ethic, but to stop taking casework home.

A short time later, he saved another child in much the same fashion as the first child. Again the mother had fished the infant out of a small wading pool. She was also so distraught that she could not tell the dispatcher if the child was breathing or not.

Ed again overheard the dispatch and responded. He again arrived before paramedics, and claimed the child had not been breathing when he arrived. He said that he started infant CPR on the child and that it started to breathe again.

Paramedics found this suspicious.

Their resuscitation rate with CPR was never as successful as Ed had been. They quietly mumbled that something was wrong with this repeated lifesaving by the enthusiastic officer. The brass pushed their suspicious complaints aside, and Ed was awarded another Lifesaving medal. He now had two in fewer than five years on the department.

Six months went by, and Ed Mascarenas was on patrol. He called on the radio one afternoon about another child he said he had watched fall into a backyard pool as he drove past a house. He had jumped out of his patrol car, hopped the fence that enclosed the backyard of the residence, and grabbed the child he said he saw fall into the pool. He said that he had started CPR, and requested immediate medical response.

He claimed the child was not breathing and that he had resuscitated it, as he had the past two victims. This time, however, things did not add up. The child was too small to have climbed into the above-ground pool, and had been left in a swing by her mother for a brief moment while the mother went into the house. She came back out to find her child was in Ed's arms, wet from the pool, and he claimed to have saved her from drowning.

They say lightning never strikes twice, but how about three times? This time, no one believed Ed. He was pissed that the tactic backfired—and now there was an investigation into the previous lifesaving events.

He was never formally charged with falsifying reports, but the rumor mill kept whispering that the lifesaving events were now being questioned and Ed was being watched. Not surprisingly, Ed never saved another infant.

Instead, he looked for other ways to shine. He eventually worked his way into the DUI squad. He volunteered to become a Drug Recognition Expert (DRE). He, along with one other officer, was sent to the DRE school, and six months later both were certified as DRE-trained and -certified officers.

His work ethic was taking its toll on his relationship with his new bride. He and Victory had been married for about a year, and they had a child on the way. It would be his second child, and her first. He worked harder to pay the bills and took whatever overtime he could.

One night he was headed home, after already having been held over for two hours , and an officer called out that he had a located a DUI and asked if Ed could respond. Ed paused and then said yes, he could. He came back to work, completed the DUI paperwork, and then signed off the radio, telling dispatch that he was done for the night.

He headed home, and about half-a-mile later he was hit broadside by another drunk driver. His left shoulder was injured in the impact, and he required medical treatment. He was about to get a reality check.

When he went to file a workers' compensation claim, the department denied it. They said that because he had signed off the radio two minutes before the crash, he was no longer at work. They would pay him no compensation for his injuries.

Ed could not believe what he was hearing. His medical bills started to pile up, and he was unable to work because of the injury.

This was the beginning of the end for Ed. As the bills piled up, he eventually lied about his condition and came back to work before his shoulder was healed.

He tried to work his way out of the bills, picking up every overtime shift he could. His new wife was mad that he was never around to help with their new child—while his ex-wife was pushing for more child support for his first child.

He was getting jammed from every angle. To make matters worse, soon after this happened, his ex-wife was charged for check fraud, and he had to take custody of their child while she served time in prison. He kept fighting back, working hard, and nursing the injured shoulder. He was under a lot of stress.

There was an apartment building in the center of the city that housed mostly poor people. Entire families would be housed in one-bedroom apartments. The building had been an upscale apartment house in the 1940s, but fifty years later it was run down and overpopulated.

One night, an elderly man was sitting in the basement of the building, in a recliner someone had thrown away. Somehow it had made its way into the basement, and it was where this man slept if he found it vacant at night.

The man was homeless. This was one of many places he had found in the inner city to stay, which was out of the elements, and relatively safe. He would sift through the cigarette butt cans outside the apartment building, looking for discarded portions of used cigarettes. One night he found several, and began to smoke in this favorite throw-away chair in the basement of the building. He fell asleep, and the cigarette fell out of his hand into the cracks of the chair's upholstery.

An hour later, he woke up to find his chair on fire. He ran from the building, but warned no one. The building was quickly engulfed.

Ed was on duty that night, and responded to the report of the fire. He and many other officers arrived and were out of their vehicles. They entered the burning building, grabbing children, old men, women, and anyone they could save, dragging them from the smoke.

Ed finally really was a hero, and the reality was painful. He and his fellow officers saved a lot of people, but not everyone. He had to stand by and listen while people screamed from inside the building as they burned to death. His shoulder had not healed, and in the rush to save people he had aggravated the injury.

I talked to him the next day, and he broke down in tears. He told me about hearing little children screaming from inside the burning building, and feeling helpless and unable to do anything while they burned alive.

His shoulder was really in bad shape now, and he asked me to tell no one how bad it really was. I agreed not to tell anyone. About a month went by, and he decided to try to get a job in another department.

This happens a lot after an incident like that fire. Cops will leave to try to get away from the memories of death. Ed was testing for the new job, and could not pass the physical because of his injured shoulder. He was really depressed afterwards, and started to drink a lot.

Soon after, he was caught drunk-driving and arrested for DUI. His medals and work ethic meant nothing now. He was a DUI enforcement officer and had been caught driving drunk. He was disgraced. He was convicted and lost the job that had meant so much to him. His new wife left him as well. His entire life fell apart in the space of six months.

He joined Alcoholics Anonymous and tried to recover his life. The last I heard, he was running a backhoe for an outdoor pool company. He was now digging the holes for installing the swimming pools out of which he had pulled the alleged drowned infants years earlier.

CHAPTER EIGHT

THE PRESTON BROTHERS

OUR DEPARTMENT HAD SEVERAL SETS of brothers working as cops. Looking back now, I recall at least five sets of brothers working for the department. But none of them were more dysfunctional than the Preston brothers. They are great examples of amazing cops who went down in flames.

The Preston brothers were as different as night and day. Mike, the older one, was tall, thin, and had a head full of dark hair. He loved attention, loved to party, and went to all the department functions. Scott, the younger one, was stocky, athletic, had thinning hair, and was edgy as hell. He hated parties. He trusted and socialized with no one. Both were gifted in their own way. Here are their stories:

MIKE PRESTON

Mike Preston had one major goal as a kid. He wanted to be a cop more than anything. He watched every Dirty Harry Callahan movie, every John Wayne movie, and every cop show there was to watch on TV. He had to become a cop; it was an obsession. But he had some very serious obstacles to overcome to make that goal a reality.

First, Mike and Scott were both raised poor in the city in which they worked. That meant baggage from inner-city life. Mike was a high-school dropout. At seventeen, he had been kicked out of every high school within driving range for fighting and failure to attend classes. He could not overcome the demons of his childhood. Angry and looking for a face to smash so he could vent his anger, he fought all the time, and when there was no one to fight, there was always his favorite punching bag: his brother Scott.

At twenty-four, Mike decided it was time to turn his life around. He was working as a gas-station attendant for minimum wage. He had not graduated high school. He had an arrest record for drugs. He was married to a woman he had met at a drag race in which he was driving, and he had impregnated her with one of the five illegitimate children he would eventually sire. But in spite of all that, he decided one day to try to become a cop.

If he had had any idea what a long shot it was for a convicted drug grower and user to become a cop, he would have tried for something else. But he had no idea that people who get arrested for drugs never make it as cops. So he charged forward.

To make a very long story short, he amazingly overcame all those obstacles. He had his criminal record expunged, obtained his GED, he divorced the crazy drag-racing groupie he'd married, and through a series of incredibly lucky breaks became a cop in the city in which he and his brother Scott had grown up.

In his mind, Mike had arrived. He had dug himself out of a crushing hole of poverty and no future and had become a cop. He bought a used Corvette to reward himself.

He worked all the overtime shifts he could get, and saved up for his dream house in the mountains above the city. He was not a good father, or a good husband. But he had achieved his childhood dream of being a cop.

His father was immensely proud of Mike, his oldest son, and of his accomplishments. He bragged about him often at the coffee shop in the afternoons, after work, and on the weekends.

One day Mike's dad had coffee at his favorite coffee shop with a man who was also a cop.

"Do you know my son, Mike? If so, what do you think of him?"

"You should be proud of him. Mike is an outstanding rookie and a bright star in the department. Mike has some issues, he has a hard time controlling his anger, and the department has taken his nightstick away for excessive force, but overall he is going to be a solid cop…someday."

Mike's dad beamed with pride at this report on his oldest son. Think of how he felt, knowing his oldest son was a cop in the city in which he had raised him. He could not have been more proud of his son and all that he had overcome to get where he was.

Mike paid his dues in patrol. He handled calls like the rest of the rookies. He had a few bumps along the way, and nearly lost it all when one day a senior patrolman suddenly remembered who Mike really was. Mike had a past in the city as a drug user and a street cruiser who did nothing but look for fights. Mike told me one night while we sat and talked in a parking lot that one day a senior patrolman suddenly remembered the loser version of Mike and remembered that he had been arrested for growing pot in his apartment. This should have shown up on his background investigation when he was hired, but it had not.

The hunt was on. The senior patrolman was out to rid the department of Mike and shatter his dream of being a cop. Mike told me that he was seriously worried that his past had come back to haunt him. He was called in to the administration and had to meet with a crusty old lieutenant, who also was in charge of the computer and records section for the department.

The lieutenant had already discovered that Mike had expunged his arrest record. He had access to the state file at an admin level, which granted him unlimited access to the records. He asked Mike to explain the arrest.

Mike admitted that he was really scared. His dream was slipping away, but he came clean and told the lieutenant everything—all of it, more than was even in the files. The lieutenant was impressed by his honesty, and thought it over. This was before software had the ability to track a user's action in a program, and when he'd finished thinking about it, the lieutenant simply deleted Mike's arrest and conviction record, and then told him to act like this had never happened. Mike never saw his records deleted; they just never existed. *Understood?*

Mike understood. His dream had been saved, and he never forgot the gift he had been given. Mike told me of the incident and how he could not believe his luck. This couldn't happen today, but in 1985 it was possible, and did happen. The witch-hunt stopped and Mike continued on with his career.

Mike had a passion. Like every other cop in this book, he was exceptional at something. In Mike's case, he was exceptional at finding stolen bicycles.

To understand Mike's passion you had to know his history. For most of us at the department, Mike's passion was a mystery, so I asked Scott, his brother, why Mike was so determined to locate every stolen bike in the city. Scott rolled his eyes.

"You have to understand, Mike had a bike when he was thirteen years old. He saved all his money and bought the bike of his dreams—a Schwinn Continental. He had it for about one month, showing it off to the whole neighborhood, and then one day it was stolen from behind our garage."

Mike blamed Scott, of course. He said Scott had left the bike lock undone, and that the Hispanic family across the street must have taken it. Mike was pissed beyond belief, and heartbroken.

Their dad also thought one of the Hispanic kids must have taken it. At the time, Scott was hanging out with one of that family's kids, and he invited him over for dinner and to play basketball, much to his dad's disapproval. When the bike was stolen, Mike's dad confronted the eight-year-old Hispanic boy, and told him that he could no longer come over to play with Scott.

"I know that you had something to do with stealing Mike's bike and you are no longer welcome here," Mike's dad said. The boy tried to explain that he had done nothing, but there was no reasoning with the older man.

I asked Scott, "Are you serious? This is why he has made it his mission in life to recover stolen bikes?" I mean it was an obsession—Mike was ridiculed by all the other cops, and even the dispatchers had assigned him the unofficial call sign of "BIKE-ONE," mocking his unrelenting mission to find stolen bicycles.

Scott replied, "Yep that's it. That's the reason why. The funny thing is, thirty years later I actually found out who *did* steal the bike."

Scott said, "I was working an event for overtime pay, and I was talking to one of the DJs at the event. The DJ and I had grown up in the same neighborhood and we remembered each other. We started talking, and out of nowhere, the DJ admitted to stealing Mike's bike."

Scott said that the DJ had been arrested several times as a kid for breaking into homes and stealing items. He said that the DJ gave a detailed account of stealing the bike and selling it, and then using the money to buy pot. The DJ laughed at how heartbroken Mike had been and said, "That's what he gets for showing off his bike, the arrogant dumbass."

"So now you know the reason for the unrelenting search for stolen bikes by 'BIKE-ONE.' Mike wanted to try to make sure that he did what he could to get back every stolen bike for every kid in the city. It was a personal goal for him to make a difference to the kids."

Mike had a few assignments in the department, but for the most part, aside from catching bicycle thieves, he was not very motivated. He had a reputation for doing the absolute bare minimum to get by. He tried out for Motors, but was rejected.

He tried out for SWAT and was rejected. He tried out for Detectives and Gangs and was rejected. He tried out for K-9 and dropped out after one day because it was too much work. He tried out for Narcotics over and over again, and after several rejections, was finally was accepted. He made the most of Narcotics, and afterwards spent the majority of the time remaining in his career in patrol.

In patrol, Mike had a reputation for not showing up on calls to which he'd been assigned. He would say on the radio that he was at the call, and a few minutes later claim that he had been unable to locate the problem or the person who called, and would go back to routine patrol.

In reality, he would not even have started his car or moved an inch. Yep, he was a real go-getter. He could not figure out why, after several days of not showing up on calls during his shift, the sergeant went ballistic and started making the entire squad toe the line.

To Mike, it was a mystery why the sergeant was so upset. His sergeant was named Kenny Duke, and the entire shift gave him the nickname the Mad Monk for his unexplained crackdown on the squad. Duke later told me why he had to crack down. It was Mike and his lazy work ethic. Sergeant Duke wanted to make it very clear that if you were assigned to his shift, you would be working and patrolling the streets, not sleeping in the cemetery at night, answering calls on the radio only.

Another incident involving Mike happened one day in the south end of the city. Speeders were frequent in an affluent area, and BIKE-ONE was assigned to run radar there. Mike was doing this, and catching speeders at a pretty good rate. One of the people he caught was a law student who lived in the area. The law student decided to warn his neighbors of the speed trap set up by Mike. He made up a sign that said "Speed Trap Ahead," and stood a couple hundred yards down the road from Mike as he ran radar.

Most cops would have used the sign to their advantage, and mention it on the tickets they gave out. In court, it would work to the cop's advantage that the speeders ignored the speed-trap sign and continued to speed. BIKE-ONE, however, did not see it that way, and told the law student he had to leave the area and take his sign with him. The law student disagreed. He believed he had a right to free speech, and he was standing on public property. He refused to leave, disobeying BIKE-ONE.

I don't know what happened after that. The scene went to shit; a fight broke out. Mike ended up choking the student until he fell unconscious to the ground; afterwards, the guy ended up in handcuffs and on his way to jail. I guess the student had never watched the Dirty Harry or the John Wayne movies that Mike had.

The student sued Mike and the police department, and, after brief negotiations, the city settled out of court. Mike somehow kept his job, and Scott had to put up with constant teasing from the other cops about his brother's exploits.

Mike wasn't always doing things that made you wonder what the hell he was thinking, though. One night he got a call to a suspicious circumstance in an apartment building. He arrived and, unlike the usual Mike routine, he actually started to dig. He found out that a woman had been kidnapped and held against her will by a man in the apartment building. The man suffered from schizophrenia and had repeatedly raped and beaten the woman for days. He intended on killing her when he was done with her.

Mike figured out where she was, and was able to rescue her from the mentally ill assailant. Basically, Mike saved the woman's life by doing what he had dreamed about his entire childhood: being a good cop. This was, however, an anomaly. Mike had worked hard to *become* a cop, and liked the idea of *being* a cop, but he usually didn't want to put in the work required to *stay* a cop, and a good one.

Eventually, Mike's lazy ways caught up with him when he stopped a guy for drunk driving. He had the guy perform the usual FSTs (field sobriety tests), and he failed them all.

Mike checked his watch; it was nearly time to get off shift, and he did not want to spend the extra time it would take to process a DUI and complete the paperwork. So, Mike being Mike, he told the guy to walk it off—take a hike and not come back to his car for a while.

In Mike's defense, this would have been an accepted practice twenty years before, when he had started his career in law enforcement. Today, however, it is not. Today it is considered dereliction of duty. Mike didn't care; Dirty Harry wouldn't waste his time on a mere DUI, so why should Mike?

Mike left the area after making sure the guy had indeed left his car and started to walk away. What Mike didn't know was that the guy died a short time later from the alcohol and drugs that were in his system. He was way too drunk to be out walking, driving, or doing anything without supervision. Mike had been negligent, and the department administration was fed up. He was told to resign or be fired.

He resigned, and ended what he, at least, thought had been an amazing career. Mike did make a difference to those who had their bikes stolen, and he did save a kidnapped women's life, so I added him here.

SCOTT PRESTON

Forget everything you know about Mike. Scott was the exact opposite. You could not have found two more different people raised by the same parents. Where Mike had to overcome the obstacles of not graduating high school, his narcotics arrest record, and a small gaggle of children trailing behind him, Scott had one major obstacle to overcome that haunted him his entire life. No matter where he went, or what he did, Mike had been there first—and, as you can imagine, made quite the impression.

Scott grew up in the same environment but had no aspirations to be a cop. In fact, as much as Mike loved the idea of being a cop, Scott hated it. Scott grew up hating any authority figure. It was not that hard to figure out why, and probably to be expected, given that every authority figure he came in contact with thought they knew exactly what to expect from him based on their experience with Mike. To understand why Scott hated cops so much and yet became one, you have to, as usual, understand his story.

Scott rarely talked to anyone about himself. He hated attention of any kind—again, just the opposite of Mike. Eventually though, I was able to gain his trust, and one day he opened up (just a little bit) about his strange hatred of cops and why he worked as one anyway. Here is what he told me:

When Scott was maybe six or seven years old, the Watts riots were raging in California, and he watched on TV as a city was set on fire. He said he asked his mom why people were doing that. She replied that they were mad about how they were being treated, so they fought back against the people they saw as being in charge.

Scott understood this at a gut level. It seemed to his seven-year-old mind like everyone in charge was an obstacle to him being happy, because they had already established in their minds who he was before he ever met them. Scott watched the rioters and thought, "So that's how I fight back?"

The next day, he and some friends were playing on a corner when one of the city cops drove past. The cop stopped and waved. Scott unleashed all of his frustration on the cop, and started calling him names and throwing rocks at the police car. The cop was dumbfounded, and then really pissed off. He jumped out and started to chase Scott and his friends. He didn't catch them, and Scott said that for the first time, he felt empowered. It felt great to fight back against "them," the authority figures.

Several weeks went by, and Scott was on the same corner, playing alone. A car pulled up and he looked up. It was the cop he had thrown rocks at a couple of weeks earlier. The cop got out of the police car and said, "Hey kid! Come here for a minute."

Scott could tell by the cop's body language he was angry. Scott stood his ground, already stubborn beyond belief. The cop grabbed him and beat the hell out of him, right there on the corner, in broad daylight.

Scott said that all he could do was try to cover his face to protect it from the blows raining down on him—and then suddenly he was air born, flying through the air into a nearby shrub. The cop got back in his police car and left. Scott said it took him several minutes to get out of the shrubs, as he was pretty badly beat up.

The incident left an impression on him. Cops were the enemy, one of many enemies in his life. Scott said that as an adult, he understood that he had caused the incident, but he still hated cops, period. I was stunned at the story but even more perplexed at how this angry kid had become a cop himself.

Scott said that he had gone into the military after high school, and that the recruiter he talked to showed him a recruiting video of a military cop working on a base. The cop had complete autonomy, and was basically left alone unless something went to shit. Then he would arrive at the scene, deal with the problem, and leave. Basically, the cop was in charge, and no one was in charge of *him*.

Something clicked in Scott's head. Here was the answer he was looking for. Instead of always fighting authority figures, he would *become* an authority figure. He signed up and spent the next six years in the military as a military cop. The fit was perfect. He had found his niche. A huge contradiction …a cop who hated cops. But it worked for Scott.

Scott excelled in the military, and for the first time in his life he was out from under Mike's toxic shadow. Scott received a couple of medals for excellence, and two early promotions. When his enlistment was up, Scott came home and jumped through the hoops required to become a civilian cop. But he had forgotten what it was like to be in Mike's shadow, and was soon to get a reality check.

Everywhere he applied for cop jobs he had to answer the question, "Are you related to Mike Preston?" When he answered yes, the interview would go south, and it would be obvious that he was not getting hired. But Scott was determined to prove himself.

Eventually, he was hired—by the *same* department where Mike was. Scott said that he purposely chose to apply there to show everyone that he was not Mike. That there was one Preston who would work his ass off, and do more than talk.

Where Mike applied and was rejected for almost every specialty in the department, Scott doubled down his efforts and did get accepted onto the SWAT team. He was a K-9 handler as well. He got assigned to Detectives, and also had a very intense and productive run in the Gang unit. Scott hopped from specialty to specialty; some units even tried to recruit him into their unit. The narcotics sergeant and lieutenant both asked him to come to their strike force; he told me he'd refused.

Scott felt, as I did, that the narcotics unit had been compromised, and that there was too many information leaks that could only be coming from the unit itself. The lessons of childhood had taught him to rely only on himself and to be wary of his peers. He still did not trust cops, and probably never would.

Scott received medals for his actions on dangerous calls. Again, he was the polar opposite of Mike and his infamous fight with the speed-trap-sign holder. Scott excelled at almost everything he did as a cop.

Scott had a pretty successful career, and was doing pretty well as a loner. He was even recruited by the SWAT team commander after he had left the unit and asked to return to SWAT after he was witness to a drive-by shooting. Scott caught the suspects after a high-speed chase across the city, and they were later convicted. Scott didn't end up rejoining the SWAT team, however, because he did not want the event to be exploited by the team commander. He just wanted the unsolicited attention to go away. He really did not like to be singled out or recognized for his work. He just wanted to make a difference, but to do it quietly.

I did notice that Scott had an unusual gift on the streets. He could remember peoples' faces and names after a brief conversation with them, and he could still recall them years later. I asked him about it one night, and in usual Scott fashion, he denied knowing what I was talking about. I pressed him about it, and eventually he opened up a bit.

Scott said that he and his brother Mike both actually had some pretty serious talents that no one knew of. Mike had been tested by the school district when he was younger after a teacher claimed he was mildly mentally challenged. The school district brought in their resident expert on intelligence testing, and tested the allegedly mildly retarded child.

Several hours later, the expert emerged and told Mike's anxious father the news. He explained the tests and what they were designed to measure. He then dropped the bomb on Mike's father: Mike had tested incredibly high on the intelligence test. So high, in fact, that he was rated in the middle of the genius category. Scott said his dad still beamed with pride when he told this story at family gatherings. Mike was a genius—a lazy, legend-in-his-own-mind genius. Mike had unlimited potential and never used it. I could see this irritated Scott unbelievably.

"So what was *your* gift, then?"

He tried to avoid the question, but eventually admitted it was both a gift and a curse. I asked again, "What is it?"

"You've already noticed my memory. It's true I remember people and names, but I also remember situations and scenarios. I'd conduct interviews in the Gangs unit and in Detectives, and write the reports later entirely from memory, in incredible detail. I could actually remember the case numbers of cases years later. Street addresses, phone numbers, names and case numbers all stuck in my head, along with names and faces."

"I can see that this is an amazing gift. So what's the curse?"

Scott sighed and said, "That same recall and memory make it impossible to forget the really bad shit we see. Think about that. I can't pick and choose what I remember; I remember it all—every dead child, every rape victim, every fatal car crash, every murder victim, and every real asshole we meet. I can't go anywhere and not see people I know from work. I know details about them, good and bad. Get it? There is no escape. I take this shit with me everywhere I go. On the streets, that memory works for me. I can find people, remember their names, who their family members are and what they've done, but I can't shut it off."

I had never thought about memory that way before. No wonder the dude was so fucked-up and edgy.

Here is an example of one incident in which I know Scott was involved. He mostly worked alone, and spent a lot of time talking to people on the streets. He believed strongly that he could learn from anyone, and treated everyone with respect until they forced him to do otherwise.

Scott was intensely interested in the city's raging gang problem. There was one dominant gang in the city at the time, and it was running the patrol officers ragged. Scott spent a lot of time talking to this gang's members, learning who was in charge, how plans were made by the group, who called the shots. All of this information he passed on to the gang-unit detectives.

One night, Scott found out that the gang leader's mother desperately wanted her son out of the gang. Scott was able to spend an hour or so talking to her, and realized that here was the veteran gang leader's weak link. He loved his mother more than anything.

It took several weeks of talking to the jaded gang member, but Scott was able to convince him to give up the internal workings of the gang. In exchange for immunity against any pending criminal charges, the gang leader spilled his guts. He sat in interviews with the gang-unit detectives for hours, discussing details, tactics, and plans that had been made.

Afterwards, the sergeant of the gang unit made a point of thanking Scott. Scott said that the sergeant told him that he had a rare talent for reaching people and talking to them as human beings instead of as criminals. The sergeant said that he greatly appreciated the efforts Scott had made, and was going to recommend him for an award.

Scott heard the word *award* and knew that meant attention. He asked the sergeant not to do what he was planning; Scott did not want the attention. The sergeant was baffled—most cops crave attention. Scott's brother Mike would have jumped at the chance for his peers to see him given an award.

The sergeant shook his head and said, "Okay, I'll do as you ask. You really are different from your brother. Are you sure you're not adopted?"

Scott smiled and said, "I've often wondered that myself."

Some nights, Scott and Mike would work overlapping shifts. On rare occasions they would get a call together, which almost always ended badly. Here are a couple of examples to show you how different they really were:

One night the two brothers were sent to respond to a report of a family fight in progress. They both arrived at the lower west-end residence and started to ask questions and take statements from witnesses.

They eventually determined that a fight had occurred at the house, but they could not figure out who was at fault.

The laws governing domestic violence were in a constant state of flux at the time. This was about ten months after the OJ Simpson trial, and the state legislature was still tweaking the domestic violence laws in a desperate attempt to deal with that continuing hot issue.

Both the husband and wife involved in the dispute to which the Prestons had responded had signs of injuries. Obviously a fight had occurred; however, at the time, the laws required the cops themselves to determine who the predominant aggressor was and arrest that person.

In this case, there was no clear sign of which party was the predominant aggressor. Mike asked the husband to step out of the house and into the front yard while another officer spoke to the woman involved. Mike, Scott, and the future Sergeant Leeds surrounded the man; while Mike talked, Scott and Leeds completed a triangle around the suspect. The suspect had nowhere to go should he try to escape. At least that was the idea.

Mike asked a few probing questions and tried to get the suspect to make some kind of admission, until it became really clear that that was not going to happen.

Mike suddenly stepped out of the triangle and opened it up, leaving a huge hole that the suspect could run through should he decide to do so.

Scott was puzzled; *WTF was Mike doing?* Scott looked at Mike and saw an evil expression, familiar from when they were kids. Mike was plotting something.

The suspect saw the opening and decided to run while the opening was there. Immediately Mike smiled and let out a loud YAHHOOO! The chase was on.

Mike could have easily caught the suspect in the first ten steps, but hung back a little. Scott was behind him, and wondered what the hell Mike was doing. Mike said, "Let him get around the next corner before we tackle him."

Puzzled, Scott waited till they turned the corner, and then Mike sped up and tackled the suspect. A normal arrest would have involved the two cops grabbing the guy's arms and handcuffing him, but Mike had other ideas.

Scott grabbed an arm and brought out his handcuffs. Mike said, "No not yet; don't cuff him."

"Why?"

"Because I'm not done kicking his ass yet!" And Mike started raining down punches on the guy's head.

Scott looked at the smile on Mike's face, and remembered seeing that smile his whole life when Mike got into fights. This was bullshit. Scott stopped the abuse, and handcuffed the suspect.

He and Mike were instantly in each other's faces, old rivalries reborn. The two cops nearly came to blows, exchanging insults and shoving each other. It was plain to Leeds, when he turned the corner, that something had happened between the two brothers, but he was much slower than they were and had missed the incident after the suspect was tackled.

Mike called Scott a rookie and said he had a lot to learn about the streets—his favorite insult. Scott told him never to pull shit like that again. The two brothers departed the scene, and did not speak to each other again for years.

Another night Mike was dispatched to an aggravated assault in progress. Right after he received the call, he signed out to attend to a parking problem in a grocery store. Yep! Mike put the felony in progress on hold because there was a parking problem in a grocery store that needed immediate attention.

That is what seasoned veteran officers do, right? They see the bigger picture, realizing at any moment the parking problem could get out of hand—and who knows what could happen then?

The dispatcher was quite understandably pissed off. It was a summer night, and there were no other units available to handle the aggravated assault in progress. Everyone was tied up on other calls, except the seasoned veteran Mike. The dispatcher ridiculed Mike for choosing to see to the parking incident first, and tried to get him to take the call, but he would not.

I was with Scott on another call, and he was pissed off immediately. Hearing the exchange between Mike and the dispatcher, he turned to me and said, "Can you believe this shit? You watch, tomorrow he'll tell our family about how he saved some guy's life, or rescued some kid from a fire. You would not believe the bullshit he tells our parents."

"Do they know about how he is called BIKE-ONE?" I asked.

Scott laughed and said, "No, and I don't have the desire to tell them. Mike is my dad's favorite; he walks on water as far as the old man is concerned."

Scott got on his cell phone and told dispatch that he would take the call for the aggravated assault in progress. The call we were on was nearly complete, so he left while I finished up. So Scott went, without backup, on the aggravated assault call, while Mike handled the more important parking problem.

After Scott arrived, secured the scene, requested medical assistance for the injured victim, arrested the suspect, and was nearly ready to leave the scene, Mike suddenly sounded off on the radio. He was clear of the parking problem and said he was now able to handle the aggravated assault. The dispatcher told him the call had been handled by Scott. Mike just said, "Okay, then I'm available to handle calls." The dispatcher said nothing. Yep, Mike was available—till another dangerous parking problem arose.

I asked Scott, "How the hell are you two brothers?"

Scott rolled his eyes. "I've always wondered," he said.

Scott continued quietly collecting awards and tried to stay below the radar. He had his own demons to deal with. He had been married several times and could not seem to find the same success in his personal life as he was enjoying at work. He had three kids, and was a great father. His kids were his hope for the future. He told me once that his life-long goal was to make sure that his children never had any idea what it was like to grow up like he and Mike had.

He did not succeed in being a decent husband, however. On his third marriage, buried in debt from divorce, Scott started to fall apart. The inability to shut down the bad memories from work, and the stress of divorce and debt, started to take their toll. Scott was a loner, and had no outlet for the stress. He worked out feverishly and tried to use the old tricks that had made his life bearable. Eventually, though, it all fell apart.

Scott had married a woman he met while working a part-time job, and they had moved into a place in the city. Scott was working two jobs and all the overtime he could scrape up to pay the bills. One night he discovered that his new wife had been having an affair with her boss and her boss's husband. Scott was devastated, and he went after the couple with whom his wife had betrayed him.

Scott had a battle plan on the streets. He employed psychological warfare against the hardcore criminals he went after. Upping their stress level making them worry where he was, what he knew, and how he would next come after them. He used this same tactic on the adulterous boss and her husband.

This time, however, it backfired. His wife's boss went to the police department and complained. An investigation took place, and Scott was found clearly to be in the wrong. He was given a choice by the department: he could resign, or face public humiliation. The investigators told him they would be forced to release to the press the fact that he had been involved in the incident and had terrorized his wife's lovers. More attention was the last thing Scott wanted, and the choice was obvious. He resigned from the department.

Scott had an amazing career that any cop would envy. Multiple assignments, awards, and recognition, and he truly made a difference on the streets. But his personal life was a mess, and it destroyed his career.

Scott pressed on and recovered financially. He was hired again as a cop, but he never again made the impact on the streets that he had when he was with our department. Scott did a lot that will never be recognized. Years after he left the department he would get phone calls about cases he'd handled and questions about what he was doing now. We kept in touch, and I know that he won't like being added to this book. Too bad.

CHAPTER NINE
PAUL BAILEY

PAUL BAILEY GREW UP IN the inner city, and was a gifted athlete from the time he was a small boy. He was a star on his high school basketball team. He played the forward position, and was a huge reason for the team getting to the state championship his senior year. In the final state game, with three seconds remaining, the point guard passed Paul the ball, and he took the go-ahead winning shot; the ball passed through the rim and made the familiar *swish* you hear when it touches nothing but net. The team had won their first state championship in twenty years. Paul was the hero of the game.

Paul's life was like that—charmed. He secured a full ride scholarship to the local college and completed his four-year degree. While in college, he married his high school sweetheart. She was a gifted athlete as well, and played high school and college basketball. They both graduated from college with academic and athletic honors. They were two gifted and talented people making their life's dream a reality.

After college, Paul decided that he wanted to be a cop. He looked at all the local police and sheriff's departments and decided to go with the sheriff's department.

He had an intense love of hunting, and working at the sheriff's department enabled him to patrol large areas of the county. He was in fact scouting future hunting spots almost daily while he worked, patrolling the large areas of heavily wooded mountain land. Athletics had taught Paul that when there was an opportunity, you had to strike while the iron was hot.

Paul lived his life like that, sometimes making impulsive decisions that he would later regret, because he thought he saw a once-in-a-lifetime opportunity.

Paul hunted every hunting season in his state, and often would travel to Alaska to hunt and fish there as well. He lived to hunt and fish.

Paul's other passion was being a cop. He loved the job. He excelled at law enforcement and held several specialties while he was employed by the sheriff's department. He was selected for the warrants division, and was recognized for his ability to locate and apprehend the most difficult-to-find criminals. Serving warrants came as second nature to him. He said it was like hunting, and he excelled at it, making it a personal quest to "track" and "hunt" the more elusive bad guys. That was his mindset. The more intense the challenge, the more he immersed himself in it. He was truly exceptional.

After his assignment in the warrants division, he was assigned to the civil division. His talent in hunting down and locating people would be an asset there as well, and the division commander realized that immediately. Paul continued to shine in the department.

Paul had never had a goal that he did not achieve. Everything that he set his sights on, he achieved. Both at work and in his hunting, he set goals and then pursued them with a single-minded obsession until the goal was achieved. He had been all over North America, hunting and killing various trophy animals. When he set out on a trip, he almost always returned with his hunting tag filled and another animal to take to the taxidermist.

There was one animal that had eluded him over and over again. That was the large male black bear. Paul had tried and failed several times to hunt and kill a black bear. It was a tough prize to locate, and it tormented him.

One year Paul and several other deputies had planned a deer hunt. They had scouted the area they planned to hunt and obtained the necessary tags enabling them to hunt legally. They were all cops, and made sure that they hunted by the state fish and game rules. They always hunted on land that they had obtained permission to be on, using legal methods to kill the desired trophy. On this particular hunt, they had set up camp and had decided to go out early the next morning. They set out topographic maps and planned the next day's hunt. They went to sleep early after drinking beer by the campfire and eating dinner.

The next morning they set out and began the long trek through the ravines and mountain passes to get to the really big trophy bucks. They had walked about an hour when Paul spied his most elusive prize—the black bear.

He saw a huge male black bear, and it was unaware of his presence. He got closer, and his goal-driven, strike-while-the-iron-is-hot mentality took over. He later said that he knew he would never again get an opportunity to hunt and kill a black bear this size.

He raised his rifle, quietly breathed in and out, held his breath while squeezing the trigger on his 30-06, and shot the huge bear. He killed it with one shot. Finally, his goal had been achieved! Paul was elated. He yelled out with incredible joy, screaming and ranting. It was a moment of pure *fiero*, the Italian word for the primal and visceral gut reaction someone has when they finally achieve a long-sought-after goal.

Paul finally has his victorious kill, and his cop friends came running, thinking he had bagged a huge buck. There was absolute silence when they arrived and found the excited and overjoyed Paul standing over the monster bear with a huge smile on his face.

They all knew black bear was not in season. This was an illegal kill. It was a crime to poach any animal out of season, and here they were, all sworn police officers, witness to another cop committing a crime. Paul had put them all in a pretty shitty predicament with his win-at-all-costs mentality.

There was a long and heated argument about what to do with the bear. Paul intended on keeping it no matter what. He wanted to have it mounted and added to his other trophies. In the end, after a long and heated argument, Paul kept the bear and brought it back to the city.

That long-desired bear would be the end of Paul Bailey's career.

He had a friend who was a taxidermist, and he asked him to mount the bear. This put his taxidermist friend in a bind as well. He could lose his license to do business and be charged criminally as well if he did as Paul requested.

Rumors began to travel around the sheriff's department about the bear, and eventually Paul learned the truth about secrets. A secret is only truly a secret if only one person knows it. When two people know, it's no longer a secret. Paul had no way he could keep the bear he'd illegally killed a secret. Either his taxidermist friend or one of his cop hunting buddies turned him in.

Eventually his illegal killing of the black bear was found out by fish and game cops (we called them fish dicks then, and still do). He was criminally charged as a poacher, and had to resign as a cop.

The account of his poaching charge was printed in the local newspaper, and he had to live with the public humiliation of failure for the first time in his life.

CHAPTER TEN
WILLIAM ROSS III

WILLIAM ROSS III WAS ONE of the most amazing hero-to-zero stories I ever witnessed. Next to Robert Suggs, he was the single most eye-popping example of a cop-gone-bad I have ever seen. This is his story.

William Ross III was hired as a cop in the city when I was just entering the military. He paid his dues on the streets and excelled as a cop, learning the ins and outs of the legal system and the courts.

He decided early in his career that he wanted more than the life of a cop. He knew that he was "better" than the life he was living. He deserved more money, more respect, more of everything—period. He would not be spending the rest of his life hauling piss-soaked drunks to jail and fighting it out with thugs in bars.

William knew he was more than he appeared to be to his fellow cops. He was smarter than they were, and he just knew he was better than they were as well. He saw a brighter future, and he was hell-bent on obtaining it. He enrolled in night classes and began the long and arduous process of obtaining his degree while working shift work as a cop.

I arrived back in the city several years later. I did not know William at the time, but I had heard his name mentioned in conversations with other cops. By that time, William had finally made it. He had worked his way off the streets and had passed his bar exams. He was now a lawyer, and was making four or five times the income he would ever have earned as a cop. The other cops were envious, and some were outright jealous to be sure—though I did hear one old-timer say, "I don't envy him at all; all that money will come back to haunt him."

The other cops laughed at the veteran cop and made fun of his simple remark. He replied, "You all know what we see every damn night. The very rich are no better off than the very poor." He continued, "I'll be surprised if all that money doesn't ruin his life." I thought about that and wondered.

A couple of years later I was called to William's new house on a report of prowlers. I parked a block away and walked in. After I confirmed that the prowlers had left, I met him in the darkened driveway. We walked around his luxurious new house with a flashlight, checking to see if anything had been stolen. We walked together, talking quietly as we checked the grounds. William had bought a piece of land on this, the most recent street to be cut into the mountains high above the city.

His house was the last house on the street, and had manicured grounds and low-voltage lighting along all of the walkways. He paid a gardener to maintain the grounds, and kept two huge Rottweilers as guard dogs for the estate. He had a huge Bayliner boat, a motor home, and a decked-out Jeep CJ. He proudly showed me all of his beautiful new possessions as he told me that he, too, had once been a cop, but had worked himself out of the job and into the courts as an attorney.

He said, "I used to be one of you, I know what it's like on the streets, but that life was not for me. I had greater aspirations, but I still keep in touch with what is going on in the streets." I smiled and listened.

When we finished and found nothing was missing, I left his immaculate house. I would never lay eyes on him again. I did, however, follow the events of his life.

While I was driving away I thought of how it was curious that, no matter what happens to cops, they always seem to identify most with their time spent in the streets. Some cops get promoted and become administrators, and no matter how much time will have passed since they actually worked the street, they think that they're still a part of it. Here was William, living in a million-dollar home, surrounded by the best that he could purchase, and he still felt the need to make sure I knew he had not lost his edge and was "in touch with the streets." Yeah, right.

Any good cop will tell you that once you leave the streets, even for a moment, you lose touch. It is a constantly changing and dynamic environment. If you are not constantly aware and listening, just one slip-up and your arrogant ass is dead. These administrators and lawyers no longer had any idea what the streets were about.

The next day, the shift sergeant invited me to lunch and asked me to meet him at one of the nicer restaurants on the west side of the city. I walked in and was immediately struck by how beautiful the hostess was. I could go on and on about her. The truth is that words cannot describe women like this. They are rare.

The sergeant was watching me and smiled, waving me to his table. After we had ordered lunch, he said, "I heard you were dispatched to William Ross's home last night."

"I was sent there on a prowler call, but I found nothing."

The sergeant smiled. "What did you think?"

"Of what?"

He began to fill in the blanks for me and told me about William's rise to riches.

"William married into one of the wealthiest, if not *the* wealthiest, families in the area. He went to law school and became a lawyer, but more than that, he joined the elite socialites of the area by marrying a millionaire's daughter. A lot of the things William showed you he's earned, and a lot came from his wealthy wife."

I shrugged. It didn't really matter to me how William obtained the things he owned. He still wanted me to know he was in touch with the streets while living his million-dollar lifestyle.

I told the sergeant what William had told me, and he laughed too. Then he said, "There might be more to that than you realize." I asked what he meant.

He said, "Did you notice that sweet Porsche 944 in the parking lot, with the personalized license plates?" I had; it was pristine and had a beautiful dark-red paint job.

"Why?"

"The car belongs to that hostess you were staring at when you came in here."

"No shit! How does a hostess afford a car like that?"

The sergeant smiled, "*That* is the correct question to ask." He continued, "Rumor around the restaurant is she also has a wicked cocaine habit as well. Two very expensive habits, fast cars and drugs—and she works part-time as a hostess. Tell me, Zach, how do you think she can afford either?"

The only things that came to mind were high-end prostitution or porn. I mentioned both to the sergeant. He laughed and replied, "Sure, or you are the girlfriend of a certain high-priced lawyer married to the daughter of one of the wealthiest men in the state."

The light came on. Now I knew why the sergeant had invited me to lunch at the restaurant. I watched the hostess as she continually sniffed and brushed at her irritated nose. She looked like she had a cold, one of the more subtle signs of snorting coke. I said, "Really?" I had talked to Williams wife at the house and she was amazingly beautiful as well, and the fact that this one guy has two amazingly hot women was unbelievable.

The sergeant said he had it on pretty good authority (whom he refused to name) that William had bought the beautiful hostess the Porsche and that he frequently took her on vacations to Grand Cayman Island when he went on "business trips." He also kept her supplied with cocaine. William was living large, just like he'd planned.

I was grateful for the heads up, and listened to the old timers a lot more closely from then on. They always seemed to know a lot more about what was really going on under the surface than what so-called "day-walkers" are aware of.

Several years passed, and William's beautiful girlfriend had left him—and taken the Porsche. She had married a decent guy, and they had a child. She seemed a lot happier now that she was not a coke whore for the millionaire attorney. William was still living large, and financially was very well off. But it was all a house of cards that was about to come falling down at an unbelievable rate.

The event that first started William's fall to earth occurred shortly after his beautiful hostess left him and got a life. William was boating in one of the many vacation spots he frequented with a couple of friends. The boat was clipping a long at a pretty good speed at night and, according to William, he could not see the boat he hit. He claimed the boat did not have its lights turned on, as was required by law for boating at night, and he claimed he had not been drinking alcohol. The driver of the other boat was killed in the incident, and William was criminally charged.

The charges were eventually dropped, as there was no proof of William's negligence. However, those same streets with which William claimed to be so in touch at our earlier meeting were pretty clear on the point that, in private, his "friends" said he *had* been drinking, and had been going 'way too fast, and hadn't seen the well-lit boat until it was too late. The rich have their secrets, and William had another one to add to his growing pile.

A couple of more years went by, and William Ross III was up on tax evasion charges. He had found several ways of creatively laundering his money, largely through part-ownerships in restaurants and other businesses, until the IRS came after him. William hired the best attorneys he knew, and after a brief, intense battle, the charges were dropped.

The federal government is not generally known in cop circles for being well-prepared in criminal cases. Usually they rely on plea deals and negotiations to settle these cases. William, however, felt he deserved his lifestyle, and was not about to give it up and settle without a fight. He was better than everyone else and smarter as well. He was able to beat the charges.

Third time was a charm, however, and William was up on charges again a short time later—this time for stealing nearly eighty thousand dollars from an elderly client. He had overcharged the dying client, and this time the state bar had had enough of his bullshit. William was disbarred.

William Ross III fell a long, long, way in a very short period of time. His is an amazing account of hero-to-zero. I wonder if he ever thinks back on his time on the streets and feels like he's still *in touch*? Seems to me that he's now a lot closer to the criminals he used to pursue than he realized.

CHAPTER ELEVEN

MARCUS BILKO

MARCUS BILKO WAS ANOTHER COP who felt he was destined for better things—much better things. He had aspirations from the first day on the job to be chief of his department, or possibly to be elected as sheriff.

Bilko started out on the streets, like most new cops, working patrol, writing tickets when necessary and handling calls. He quietly checked into the prerequisites for promotion, and found that a four-year degree would most certainly be required for him to reach his goals.

Bilko went to school on his time off and worked hard at maintaining a respectable grade point average. He was not the sharpest knife in the drawer, but he was damned determined to be the shiniest. That was his goal. He knew he could not be the smartest guy up for promotion; he always struggled academically, but he had other assets. He was personable in a slimy, used-car-salesmen kind of way, and he loved to be involved with the media. He used those assets to his advantage.

Bilko first worked hard to get promoted to sergeant within the department, and once he had been in the position awhile, he volunteered for the much-maligned position of public relations officer.

The public relations officer presents press releases to the media and public on high-profile cases. Sergeant Bilko had a plan to use that to his advantage.

No good cops like the press. Media, and especially reporters, are the polar opposite of cops in our society. It is the way things are designed, really. From the beginning, our society has been set up for the people to be protected from the government, represented by one type of cop or another. One of the methods of oversight to protect the people from the government is a free press. Reporters are the foot soldiers of the media.

Cops and government on one side, and the media, reporters, and press on the other. The two sides constantly at odds over one issue or another.

Once in the public relations position, Bilko was in his element. The other cops had no real use for the job, but Bilko figured that he could use his natural charm and the usually tense relationship cops were known to have with the press to his advantage.

He waited for the department's first big case, and then presented his press release. He answered all the questions the reporters asked, professionally and courteously, smiling warmly at each ridiculous question and making the reporters feel like what they were asking really mattered. In a few short minutes, Bilko was able to establish a foothold with the media. He became the media poster boy.

Reporters would call and ask his opinions of other departments' cases and of issues affecting police work. He was on the television and radio and in the newspaper almost nightly, making comments about one thing or another. It made the reporters look good to their bosses to have an "in" with the cops.

Bilko worked at his craft, practicing his speeches and sound bites in front of the mirror at home till he was able to pitch the perfect combination of verbal and non-verbal queues.

The reporters flocked to his emotional press releases like never before. Bilko made the most of this acting career, and polished his public façade to a high sheen.

He was shiny and perfect—clean, neatly cut hair, new suit and freshly pressed shirt, impeccable tie. Bilko was a welcome change from the previous crusty old veteran cops who had been "voluntold" they were to be public relations officers, toothpick hanging from yellowed teeth, addressing the female reporters in a condescending tone as "li'l missy."

Sergeant Bilko had an instant impact on his department's popularity with the press. The chief was very happy with the new relationship with the media. Sergeant Bilko soon became Lieutenant Bilko, and continued to present press releases, even after he was made the lieutenant over detectives. Eventually other departments recognized his relationship with the press, and started to recruit him quietly.

Bilko bounced from one department to another, always moving to a position with more pay and of equal or greater rank. Always doing the press releases, always in the media. Reporters followed him from department to department like teenage girls following a rock star from concert to concert, minus the panty toss.

I met Lieutenant Bilko in a training class I attended, during one of his temporary landings at a local department. He was the department's new public relations officer, and had agreed to meet and greet the officers present in the department's newly remodeled training area.

Lieutenant Bilko came in and made a point of introducing himself and personally shaking hands with every cop present. I could see from the reaction of the other cops that we all instantly felt disdain for the man. He was admin, we were working street cops. Some of us were still tired from working the mid shift the previous night and hoping to catch a few hours of sleep before training in the early morning.

Lieutenant Bilko was polished and perfect. Fit from his daily routine of racquetball and a sauna. His voice was too loud, too chipper. Soft hands firmly grasped our calloused and sometimes cut and bruised hands from the previous night's battles. No one was impressed. We were not media types. Lieutenant Bilko quickly left the increasingly hostile room, and never returned.

One day Bilko came up with the idea of posting public relations videos on YouTube. This idea would make most cops cringe. Bilko, however, obtained permission from his chief of police and forged ahead, posting over 40 (yes, 40!) videos on YouTube about various units within the department and about issues a citizen or reporter might raise about the police or police procedures.

His press buddies viewed the videos constantly, and he referred to them on the department's newly designed web page, drawing even more attention to himself and his efforts.

Oh, and who do you think had a major hand in making the department web presence a reality? Bilko, of course. He was in his element.

He was noticed and appreciated almost daily for his talents with the media and web postings. He was ready, he thought, to finally make his big push for greater glory.

The aged sheriff had decided to retire, and had announced that he did not intend to run in the upcoming county elections. The newly promoted Captain Bilko saw the opportunity he had been waiting for. He went out and got another haircut, bought a new suit, and even had porcelain veneers made so that his teeth would be perfect.

One day, Capt. Bilko called his press and media buddies and told them he had "a major announcement to make at four o'clock today." When the time came, he walked into the conference room he had rented to accommodate the large gathering of reporters, and announced that he would "humbly" be seeking the office of sheriff.

Capt. Bilko left no stone unturned in his public relations blitz. Everything was perfect. He planned to attend every event, made public appearances at local rallies for law enforcement, and made sure that he commented on controversial cases currently in the local court system.

Bilko's picture was everywhere. He pulled out all the stops and spent every dime he had to have political flyers and ads made up and distributed. He paid for at least one huge billboard along the each of the major freeways that entered and exited the county. Several commuter buses were also graced by advertisements proclaiming how, with Bilko in the office of sheriff, the criminals in the city would be less likely to victimize the citizens. He claimed he was that capable, gifted and intimidating to the criminal elements of society.

It was a media blitz that was worthy of a presidential campaign. Capt. Bilko's perfect hair, perfect teeth, and new suit were everywhere you looked in the county.

People see cops in a different light from the way they see other people. You look at a cop and you want a guy in whom you can believe and have confidence. You want someone you think can be tough enough to kick a bad guy's ass if he broke into your home and held your kids at knifepoint, but not so scary that you're not sure which is worse—the bad guy with a knife or the cop with a gun. They don't want a cop who is too pretty or too scary. Much like Goldilocks and the three bears story, day-walkers want a cop that is "just right"—pretty, but not too pretty; tough, but not too scary.

Bilko had lost sight of that reality. Maybe it was because he had spent too much time with his media buddies. I don't know. I do know that wherever he made a public appearance and spoke to people, I heard comments similar to these: "That guy is a cop? He looks like a model." "I don't think that he could fight his way out of a paper bag, He might break a fingernail."

No matter what Bilko did he could not change the public's perception of his "very shiny but not so sharp self." He poured all of his financial resources and political clout into winning the election.

On the night of the election, Bilko he was sure that he would win. There was no other possible outcome in his mind. He had dotted all the i's and crossed all the t's.

The next day, however, he was faced with a very difficult reality. Bilko had lost the election.

He was emotionally devastated. More important, he was financially ruined. Bilko had poured all of his financial resources and political clout into winning the election, but no matter what he did, in the end he could not change the public's perception of his very shiny but not-so-sharp self.

His press groupies came to him for sound bites and interviews, asking what his plans were now. He was noticeably shaken by the defeat. He said that somehow he would go on with his law enforcement career. He still felt he had a calling to be a law-enforcement officer and serve the community. He had learned his part well; the sound bite sounded great and was on the evening news.

Several months went by and the financial reality had hit Bilko hard. He could barely afford to buy food, and gas for his car. He was mad and perplexed. He could not understand how he had not been elected by the people of the county as their sheriff. Reality is a hard teacher.

Bilko was so broke, he decided to start using the city gas pumps for his own personal vehicles. Every dollar he saved would help—and besides, he rationalized, he deserved the perk for all he had done for the department.

Bilko had not been informed that there had been several thefts of gas from the city's gas pumps, and so detectives had installed hidden cameras to keep track of who was pumping gas in order to catch the thieves. Imagine their surprise when wonder boy Bilko pulled up to the pumps on his day off and filled 'er up. A very quick and surgical internal investigation was conducted, and Bilko was not only let go from his job and decertified as an officer, but was also criminally charged and publically humiliated. He fell incredibly hard and fast from the top of his public relations throne.

With no job, no career, and no retirement prospects, his future was looking pretty bleak. You would think that Bilko would be done with the media.

Nope. Old habits die hard. Once a media whore, always a media whore. Mr. Bilko was contacted by one of his reporter buddies and asked if he would consider giving an interview about his fall from grace.

The reporter did not expect much. No sane person would jump back into the public spotlight after having so loudly proclaimed that he was the answer to the escalating crime rate in the county, and then, a few months later, becoming a member of the "criminal element" he claimed was so intimidated by his mere physical presence.

Mr. Bilko, however, surprised the reporter, and proved more than willing to provide an in-depth interview. At the end of the interview, looking deeply and heartbrokenly into the camera, with tears and snot running down his face, Bilko cried and asked for the public he served to please forgive him. His perfect porcelain teeth shone in the light.

Still not the sharpest knife in the drawer, Mr. Bilko did not understand that the public had seen through his shiny disguise, even if his media groupies had not.

CHAPTER TWELVE
DAN ARNOLD

I ATTENDED POLICE ACADEMY AT a satellite location. It was located at a college that had contracted with the state police academy to provide the same courses as the actual academy, but at a remote location. The coursework and academics were the same, but they were taught by local state-certified cops.

This was where I met Dan Arnold. Dan was a state-certified arrest-control instructor, and a black belt in aikido. He was one of four local cops hand- picked by the director of the police academy to teach the arrest-control course.

On the first day of arrest-control class, we lined up in six rows, and the four veteran cops made us do pushups until we could not do them anymore. I noticed right away that none of *them* did pushups. It was not going to be a lead-by-example class. The motto of the class became, "Do as I say, not as I do."

We were "worked out" by the four cops non-stop until we all were covered with sweat and some of us puked. Dan stood with his arms folded and watched. Later, on our hourly breaks, he would take out his martial-arts staff and dance around the room in mock combat with an imaginary opponent. In the brief five-minute break, we watched him break into a profuse sweat while he defeated his imaginary foe. He was that special.

Several years passed, and I was now at the same department as the four arrest-control instructors who had worked us out years before. Dan was now one of my field training officers. He was as enthusiastic working as an FTO as he had been in the arrest control class. He offered a lot of wind, smoke, and mirrors, but not a lot of action or help.

Finally, however, Dan found his place in the department. He put in for a transfer and was granted a slot in the department's traffic division.

Traffic enforcement fit Dan like a glove. It came naturally to him. In, traffic Dan rose to the occasion like he had never done before as a cop. He applied himself almost from day one. After a brief period of time, he was recognized for his efforts in DUI enforcement, and even received recognition at the state level for the impact he had in identifying and arresting drunk drivers. From there, Dan went on to obtain the department's first Drug Recognition Expert (DRE) certification. Dan sailed through the certification effortlessly.

This was a noteworthy accomplishment. Several others had attempted to get the certification and had been unable to do so. The classes are long, and it takes a lot of determination to obtain all of the necessary real-world drug observations in the field required to get the certification. Dan was proud of his certificates, and posted them in his office. I was checking them out one day when I noticed he had a diploma that stated that he had graduated with honors with a bachelor's degree in genetic engineering. I looked at the certificate and thought, *Seriously? Genetic engineering?*

"So, do you have a Bachelor of Science?" I asked

"NO!" he said. "Rookie, can't you read? It says 'genetic engineering.'"

Rookie could read just fine. Rookie decided to write down the name of the college that had awarded the genetic engineering degree and look it up later on the Internet. Guess what the stupid rookie found out? There was no such college, ever, anywhere, period.

Bad rookie for challenging the genetic-engineer wannabe. What was I thinking? I kept that little tidbit of knowledge to myself. If others wondered about the curious degree, they would just have to check it out for themselves.

The department had an aging fleet of motorcycles that desperately needed to be replaced. Dan again stepped up to the plate and was instrumental in the department obtaining a brand-new fleet of Harley Davidson police-package cruisers.

Dan felt the best he had felt about himself in a long time. He was making a contribution that mattered to the department, and his efforts were noticed and appreciated. Finally, people respected Dan in a way he thought that he deserved. Dan spent several years in traffic and then transferred to the gang unit.

As a gang-unit detective, Dan was the go-to guy for public speaking. He could not put a case together and see it through the courts to save his life, but he could give a presentation to the public that was head-and-shoulders above those of the other detectives in the unit.

Dan excelled at public speaking. He had a natural talent for putting together PowerPoint slides and charts, and making problems understandable to the groups that contacted the department and requested informative presentations.

Dan would meet with church groups and business owners, and even gave a brief at the honors forum at the university. Day-walkers all! All totally unaware of what went on in the streets of their city at night. Dan spoke to them on a regular basis, and made problems seem less frightening, telling them we in the police department had the problems under control and well in hand. It was far from the truth of course, but it comforted them, and that was what they needed.

Dan spent a few years in the gang unit, and then was hand-picked to head up the department's newly organized intelligence unit. The unit was supposed to gather information on criminals and their activities, matching specific crimes committed to a list of criminals who specialized in that type of crime, matching MO and past history to the people. The idea was to speed up the process of identifying who had committed the crime and making an arrest.

I have no idea how Dan did at that specialty. The chief and his administration chose him specifically. Dan was selected because they thought that he could work alone and master the task at hand. The unit was quietly managed, and no one knew what really went on—probably not even the chief.

Dan, like most cops, had a few issues he kept on the down low. One day, however, he got himself into a real shit storm. Dan had been seeing a woman who was a convicted felon. This was a major faux pas for a cop, especially a veteran cop in charge of gathering intelligence on the criminal elements of the city. Dan met with her on occasions when her boyfriend was gone and "gathered Intelligence" on a pretty regular basis.

The boyfriend became suspicious that something was going on while he was away. Maybe neighbors said something, or maybe he just had a hunch. Either way, he came home early one day and caught Dan in the act of "gathering intelligence" from his girlfriend.

Dan hopped off the woman and grabbed his gun, holding the man at gunpoint. He then handcuffed him and stuffed him in a closet while he thought about what to do next. Yep, this scene went to shit in the blink of an eye. Dan was in a convicted felon's apartment "gathering intelligence," which was totally against the rules, and now he had her boyfriend at gunpoint and in a closet in handcuffs. Amazing how fast that happened.

The old cops had a saying that they repeated over and over to the new guys when I was first starting. It was pretty crude, and at the time I thought it was bullshit. But as the years went by I watched more and more of my fellow cops fall by the wayside because they failed to listen to the saying and take it to heart: "The badge will get you pussy, but the pussy will get your badge." Dan was about to find this out in a big way.

There was no way to make this little intelligence-gathering episode disappear. Next thing Dan knew, he was up on aggravated kidnapping charges and he had lost his job. He was decertified as a cop and would never work again in the field of law enforcement. The incident made the local news and then the national news. I was in another state and actually saw the incident mentioned on TV.

Somehow Dan was able to reach a deal with the prosecutors, and charges were dropped. He had reached the required time limit in the state retirement system and he was allowed to retire quietly after this very public humiliation.

He went from being handpicked to run a specialized unit within the department to being charged with a felony himself. Dan dropped from grace as quickly as his convicted-felon girlfriend could drop her panties for some "intelligence gathering."

CHAPTER THIRTEEN
CHRISTOPHER COPE

CHRIS COPE IS AN AMAZING story to me, and maybe that's because I was a part of the beginning of his incredible flame-out as he came crashing down to earth. Before I tell you about the crash and burn though, you need to know his background.

Cope joined the state patrol as an enthusiastic young rookie fresh from the state police academy. He had wanted to be a trooper his entire childhood. Some kids want to be firemen or rock stars; some dream of being professional athletes. Cope dreamed of being a state trooper.

One of the proudest moments in his life was not, in fact, graduating from high school, where he was an outstanding athlete, or from college, with his four-year degree firmly in hand. It was graduating from the state police academy, at which he distinguished himself with honors and obtained the class award for the highest academic achievement. Cope had dreamed of this moment, and now it was about to be real. In a few short days he would be assigned to a county to start patrolling its freeways. He could hardly wait to begin his field training with a seasoned trooper.

Cope was a bright and shiny new guy with a bright and shiny future ahead of him. He successfully completed his training, and was set free to patrol on his own. He was highly successful in learning the ins and outs of the interstate, and the political roadmap of the state patrol organization.

Not only was Cope academically gifted, he looked the part as well. Broad shoulders, square jaw, perfect teeth, and steely blue eyes. He stood at 6'1" and weighed about 195 lbs. He was very physically fit, and had a swagger about him when he entered any room. He was a poster-boy state trooper.

Cope decided to try to specialize and distinguish himself further by becoming an SME (Subject Matter Expert). He asked for and was eventually granted a position on the state's DUI (driving under the influence) enforcement squad.

The squad was a small unit of highly trained and motivated troopers that would be tasked with saturating an area and stopping any driver who could be DUI. The squad would swoop into the area and saturate the streets, stopping everything that moved. Every car, no matter what the occupants were doing, was a target. The tactic was questionably legal, to say the least, but it was very successful, and netted the squad an impressive record of arrest statistics.

Cope excelled in the unit, and was in the top five percent of the performers. He was living his dream, making a difference in lowering the number of drunks on the road, making his home state safe. I know that it sounds a bit corny, but this is what he had dreamed of, and now it was coming true. Cope had aspirations to move up the food chain, to sergeant, maybe, and then lieutenant; if he played his cards right, the sky was the limit.

The beginning of the end for Chris Cope was one night while the DUI squad was patrolling our city. They had arrived and begun the usual saturation of our streets, looking for DUI's and stopping every vehicle.

They were not entirely welcome in the city. They had no idea who they were stopping and what kind of danger they might have stepped into with this slash-and-burn mentality. One minute you were stopping an elderly couple on their way home from a movie, the next a carload of gang members armed and looking for a fight. That was the reality in our streets. Anyone you stopped could be your next gun battle.

We took it seriously. State troopers did not always recognize the danger of the people they stopped until they were knee-deep in shit. Cope was the exception, however. He was as sharp as any trooper I have ever met.

This particular night, Cope had a ride-along, a college student who had taken a class at the local university and elected to ride with a state trooper for the practical experience, actually seeing the job that they did from the front seat of the car.

Cope had been out on patrol about four hours with the ride-along. They had stopped and assisted two other troopers who had found DUIs, and were looking for their own when they decided to stop a car full of juveniles. The driver was a young woman who had failed to signal as she changed lanes in front of Cope and his decked-out state cruiser.

Cope called out on the radio that he was stopping the car, and gave his location. He was outnumbered, as there were at least four or five occupants, so he decided to call for backup. Cope walked up to the driver and spoke to her, asking her for license and registration. He looked around the interior of the car and later said that he got a bad feeling about the occupants. Cope obtained the documents from the driver and walked back to his car, checking over his shoulder to make sure he was not about to be ambushed.

While he ran the information, another state trooper pulled up; the two troopers talked and watched the occupants fidget inside the car. They decided that they wanted to pull the occupants out one by one from the back seat forward. Once they had most of the occupants removed, they went up to remove the front passenger. He was a Hispanic male and a gang member recently released from prison. In a short ten seconds, Cope's whole world would begin to change. The gang member had a gun and tried to shoot Cope. He failed.

Cope was highly proficient with his firearm. He was not the average trooper. He saw the weapon, immediately yelled "GUN," and pulled his own weapon. All of this was done in an instant; Cope's handgun cleared his holster less than one second after the gang member pulled and pointed his own gun. That is incredibly fast. But like I said before, Cope was no ordinary trooper. He shot several rounds into the gang member, and was able to survive the shooting with no injuries.

To make a long story short, Cope had survived an ambush. His decked-out state patrol cruiser was equipped with a dash camera, and the entire stop was recorded. Cope's tactics were by-the-numbers perfect. Soon he was well-known to the entire state patrol as one of their own who had survived street combat and done it in an exemplary fashion. Again the sky appeared to be the limit for Trooper Cope.

What no one tells you about shootings is the effect that they have on you down the road. Cop training is about surviving the moment, surviving the battle, doing it by the numbers, and if you live through the actual experience, you become one of a very small group of law enforcement officers in this country. A lot of cops are involved in shootings, and a lot die.

Unfortunately some do something in the heat of the battle that the laws of their state frown on, and that lead them to be looked at as criminals themselves. They lose everything in the brief, furious struggle to survive.

Cope survived physically, and appeared to have come out of the event emotionally stable as well. He was recognized by the governor of the state for his heroism, and given a medal at the state capital. The awards ceremony was publicized and on the evening news as well. Cope was as a recognized hero. The gang member, on the other hand, was found to be criminally responsible for the shooting and sent back to prison, still carrying one of the bullets from Cope's weapon in his chest.

Things appeared to be rolling along smoothly for Cope. He became the treasurer for the local troopers' benefit association. It was largely a political position, which was one of the many boxes to check on your way up the food chain, necessary to gain promotion in the agency.

But I think something had changed in Cope that night that he himself was barely aware of. Looking back, I'm not sure where it all started to unravel for him, but the position he took in the benefit association would be his downfall.

Cope was required to manage a pretty sizable sum of money, considering his was a volunteer position. The temptation became too much for him, and he started to skim small amounts from the bank account he managed. When he was finally caught, Cope was found to have taken over $27,000.

There would be no rescuing him from this event. He was publicly humiliated, criminally charged for the theft, and decertified as a state trooper. He could never again be a cop, anywhere, ever. His story was an amazing example of what I saw over and over again in the field. He fell in a very public manner.

I have no proof for what I believe happened to Cope, but I saw it over and over again. After a cop has been in a shooting, he or she changes mentally.

Some take more risks, feeling invincible or perhaps seeking thrills, trying to relive the adrenaline rush they experienced in the life-or-death battle. Maybe it's different for each person; I don't know. I do know that the change almost always occurs, and almost always ends their careers.

Cope's story was not over yet. Here's another example of the change that Cope experienced.

Surprisingly, Cope eventually experienced a change of heart regarding his assailant in the shooting. At the time of the shooting, he very much had an us-and-them mentality. This is very common among cops. Basically it means that we, the cops, are different from them, the criminals. Cope came to realize what any veteran cop already knows: we are all in this together. People make really bad decisions on a particular day and for a particular reason, and may never make those same decisions again. This doesn't make them bad people, but it does mean, in this context, that they broke the law. Cope got that. He came to feel it in a way he could never have understood before.

He too had broken the law by making a really bad decision regarding the benefit association's treasury. He empathized with the gang member he had shot, and actually started to petition the state parole board to release the young man. This did not make Cope popular with his former peers, or with the cops in the area. Cope didn't care. He had a different perception now of what it meant to be a part of the solution.

CHAPTER FOURTEEN
LT. JAMAL ETHAN

I WAS AT THE TAIL end of my career when I ran into Lieutenant Ethan. He was an intense, brooding guy who rarely had anything to say to anyone. Occasionally he would stop and talk to me about the assignment I was on and ask how things were going. Not that he really cared, but it was his job to ask.

Lieutenant Ethan had two very real passions. One was his immaculate black Lexus; the other was handguns. Especially high-end hand guns. If you wanted to see his brooding, moody side disappear, all you had to do was mention either the Lexus or his favorite handgun, the Kimber .45 caliber semi-auto. Lieutenant Ethan would light up, smiling, and begin to tell you his latest account of shooting on the range. Almost every weekend he took the Kimber out to do just that. He loved the gun like a K-9 handler loves his dog: they were inseparable. The only times I saw him happy and smiling were when he was talking about either the gun or the car; the rest of the time, he was surly.

Lieutenant Ethan was the supervisor of two completely different units. One was the incredibly undermanned detective unit, and the other the Community-Oriented Policing (COPS) unit. I was in the COPS unit. He was tasked with overseeing our events, and would provide feedback to the administration on what we had accomplished and future directions in which we would be headed.

The COPS unit was very dynamic and had a lot of public visibility. We did not make arrests or crunch crime in the usual manner; instead, we were proactive, and tried to find problems before they occurred and then squash them. This made our efforts hard to substantiate to the brass. It also made us very unpopular with the rest of the cops. We were warm and fuzzy with the public, while they had to battle every night. Our job was to improve the public perception of the department and of the efforts made to keep the peace, while a patrol officer's job was to step into the battle that is the streets and hold the line against criminals. So, two very different perspectives on the same community.

Being in charge of detectives can be challenging, to say the least. For the most part, they are extremely strong and driven personalities, and hate anyone to tell them what to do. They already know what to do, and yet still require oversight.

Detectives also have the really unenviable job of investigating other cops. If a cop crossed the line in our department, a detective would be assigned to investigate the situation and then provide feedback to Lieutenant Ethan and the rest of the administration as to what had occurred and what the department's liability was in the incident.

Cops are constantly being investigated for reports of abuse or misconduct that have not taken place. However occasionally, as you have seen in this book, there are some reports that come in that are so outrageous, they seem impossible. Detectives are tasked with investigating all of them, and sometimes they find that not only are the outrageous things possible, but they actually happened. Here is one example:

Michelle Romero was an outstanding K-9 handler. She had dreamed of being a K-9 handler ever since she had watched her father train police dogs as a child. Being a cop ran in the family, and she was a natural fit for the job. She had no illusions about the requirements of the job—the long hours spent training and caring for the dog, the late-night call-outs to assist with search warrants and building searches after someone had broken into a business. She had finally reached her dream of being a dual-purpose K-9 handler, and applied herself to the demands of the position with a determination that had not been matched by her peers.

She felt that she had a lot to live up to. Her dad was sort of a living legend in the local K-9 community, and she wanted to prove herself more than a match for the old man. Being a dual-purpose handler meant that she and her dog were certified in narcotics detection and apprehension of escaped criminals. This required a talented handler and an even more exceptional K-9. Both the handler and the dog are certified as a team. They must be able to work together as one unit.

Michelle and her K-9 were an incredible team, and they won awards nationwide. They were nationally recognized and certified. Michelle and her K-9 brought home trophy after trophy from police dog competitions, and more important, they never lost a case in court. The team also had the state's largest narcotics bust on record. The drugs had been located during a traffic stop Michelle had conducted after becoming nationally certified in drug interdiction techniques.

Michelle's father couldn't have been more proud of his daughter. She had truly surpassed his accomplishments as a K-9 officer, and in a short time. He felt it was a case of her taking his lessons and running with them. She was certainly a rising star in the K-9 handlers' world.

Michelle was a K-9 handler 24/7. She was obsessed with the job, and even started a Facebook page to promote the position and raise awareness for struggling K-9 programs in other departments. The page had several thousand followers.

One day she decided to make up a kick ass K-9 logo and have it printed up on t-shirts and sweatshirts. She offered them to a select few Facebook page followers as a thank-you for following and supporting the K-9 handlers in their area and nationwide.

The logo was really sweet, and I even ordered a couple of sweatshirts myself. I sent the money and waited. Nothing happened. I never received the shirts. I sent a message to Michelle and asked WTF had happened to my shirts. She said that she'd had problems with the printing company, but that the issues were resolved and my shirts were on their way.

A month passed, and still I had no shirts. I guess I wasn't the only one who was waiting: Lieutenant Ethan and his detectives had gotten wind of the problem from someone who had complained, and began an investigation.

Michelle was found to have taken in several hundred dollars in orders from around the country for the kick-ass logo she had produced and advertised on her Facebook K-9 page. Not one shirt had been printed, however, and they charged her with theft.

Michelle was an extremely gifted K-9 handler who went down in flames over a few hundred bucks. She went from hero to zero in an incredibly dumb fashion. I have to admit I am still disappointed. The shirts I never received looked awesome.

The detectives moved on to the next case, and quietly complained among themselves about Lieutenant Ethan.

Ethan was a very quiet guy, and apparently had a difficult time managing the detective unit. It was severely understaffed, and was always being criticized for being unable to keep up with the increasing demands placed on its investigators.

Apparently the detectives were less than happy with Lieutenant Ethan and his management style. He could really be a prick if he needed to be, and he drove them hard for results. To be honest, they hated him.

We in the COPS unit, on the other hand, loved him. He took care of us better than any supervisor did, before or after. I talked to Lieutenant Ethan about the K-9 handler case, and he shook his head. He was amazed at how stupid Michelle had been, and criticized her for her actions. He proclaimed loudly that it was the single stupidest thing he had witnessed a cop do in his tenure as the lieutenant of the detective division.

I thought about that. I had seen numerous cops go down in flames over the years and, in hindsight, they all seemed incredibly dumb. I knew that anyone was capable of anything given the right set of circumstances…even cops.

I mentioned this to Lieutenant Ethan, and he loudly proclaimed, "Not this cop! I ain't going down on some stupid shit like this. I did not drag my ass up the food chain to go down on some stupid shit like this."

I didn't see Lieutenant Ethan for several more weeks, as we were incredibly busy. Then one day I saw him coming out of work. He was preoccupied and acted edgy. I thought that maybe his high-maintenance girlfriend was getting the best of him. I called out, "Hey, Lieutenant, how's it going?" He waved, but made no comment. He got into his sweet black Lexus and left.

Over the next six weeks, Lieutenant Ethan was investigated for two different incidents. The first was an accusation that he had claimed time on his time card that he had not worked. That was found to be unfounded, and Lieutenant Ethan, who had been placed on administrative leave, came back to work for a couple of weeks on the night shift.

Pending the second investigation, he had been removed from his position as the lieutenant in charge of detectives, and honestly, he looked relieved. Or at least I assumed that look was one of relief—at no longer being burdened with responsibility for managing all the investigations.

But it was not that burden he had been worried about. A few weeks passed, and Lieutenant Ethan was again on administrative leave, this time on suspicion of theft. He was accused of stealing a very expensive handgun from an evidence locker. The gun was missing, and all the evidence pointed to him.

Guess what? Yep. Mr. "I'm-not-gonna-go-down-on-some-stupid-shit-like-that" went down on that very stupid shit.

Ethan was charged, and pleaded guilty to the theft of a handgun. He was in charge of the entire detective unit, and had investigated many thefts over the years. He knew the consequences of stealing a handgun, and he did it anyway.

Now he was a convicted felon, which meant he could never again legally own a handgun.

CHAPTER FIFTEEN
CASEY DAVIS

THE COMPLEX MIX OF TALENTS it takes to be a good cop is very hard to define. I have heard many blue-collar descriptions. "Sheep dogs protecting the flock from the wolves" seems to be the most popular at the moment. I have always liked what a veteran cop told me when I first started. He said, "You have to have been there to know how to get there." By this he meant that the best cops were problem children who grew up and went straight, but remembered where they had come from and had compassion for those they dealt with.

Anyone is capable of anything, given the right set of circumstances. That is a fact any cop realizes the first time he or she arrests the homecoming queen for possession of methamphetamines or, in my case, sees the sister of his best friend from high school arrested and convicted for burning her handicapped foster child alive for the insurance money. For cops, life is about reality checks. Lots of reality checks.

Anyway, police departments have long struggled with how to identify the intangibles that separate the good cops from the bad. Personally, I don't think it can be done. The original method used was to conduct a background check of the potential police officer. The idea was to send a seasoned investigator out to speak with the neighbors of a potential cop, check into his or her background, dig a little bit, contact some friends and some enemies to give the detective a feeling for what kind of person the rookie might be.

Seasoned detectives are rarely used for this task. In our department, wannabe detectives like Mike Preston got the job. Real detectives were much too busy to investigate a potential new hire, so right from the get-go the process was flawed. An idiot was sent out to sift through some new hire's personal life and determine if he or she had what it took to work the streets.

In the 70s and 80s, the police departments used the polygraph machine to assist the "detective" in weeding out the bad cops from the good. These tests have been around since the early 1920s, and there is ample evidence that they just don't work. I personally have known several people who have taken a polygraph and much later admitted they lied and defeated the test. They were deemed to have been telling the truth, and were amazed that they were not caught in their deception.

The idea that any test can measure human perceptions of what is and is not a lie is severely flawed. People are just 'way too complex, and their perceptions of what is right and what is wrong are not as solid or concrete as churches and civic leaders would have us believe.

Police departments, however, still believe strongly in the polygraph, and a lot of them use it to screen potential new hires. Personally, I think flipping a coin would be about as accurate in predicting whether or not the new recruit will be a good cop. Heads or tails really doesn't matter. You pick.

Next up in the arsenal used by the administrations of police departments to weed out the "bad seed" is the psychological exam. This is my personal favorite—take a test developed by psychologists or psychiatrists attempting to measure what it is that makes a cop a good risk for a department to hire.

Really? I could go on forever as to why I think this logic is flawed. But number one is this: What sane person straps on body armor to go to work? What sane person wears a gun, expecting to get involved in a shooting at any moment but hoping he or she won't? What sane person wears a uniform clearly identifying him- or herself as the one person (maybe the only person) in the crowd who will fight back if you try to harm any of the other persons in that crowd? What sane person takes a job enforcing the law, when the very constitution of our country protects criminals' rights and punishes cops for infringing upon them?

No sane person alive would take this job. No test can measure what passion burns inside of the man or woman who desires this job—the passion to be part of the solution and not to sit idly by and wonder, "What can I do?" This freak of nature cannot be measured by a test written in a warm office with soft hands untested by the streets. Yet police departments nationwide employ the tests, afraid to call academia on its bullshit claims to know what makes people tick.

Psychology is based on a process of self-reporting. What sociopath worth his lack of human connection is going to admit he is a bad choice? "Please don't hire me and give me all this power, Dr. Psych; I'll abuse it, and that just isn't right." Never gonna happen.

The latest weapon was developed by the government. I've read that it's used by the Israelis at the checkpoints they man in the no-man's land between the Israeli- and Palestinian-occupied territories in the Middle East. It's called voice stress analysis. To me it's just another electronic version of the snake oil sold by traveling salesmen in the old west. It's supposed to address the problem of whether or not a person is lying.

In law-enforcement circles, it's considered as solid a tool as the lie-detector test when it comes to locating the bad seed. However, even its developer has said in open court that it is not a lie detector, and should not be used as one.

I was an investigator in an alleged sexual molestation case in which a woman alleged that an apartment maintenance man had sexually abused her three-year-old daughter. Voice stress analysis was used by detectives assigned to the case, and the man failed miserably. I was asked to try to get a confession from the suspect.

He didn't confess. He told me that he had had a relationship with the woman, and that she wanted him to pay her rent and provide upgrades to her apartment in exchange for sex. He had initially agreed to the arrangement, but later changed his mind. He said she threatened to set him up and call the cops if he failed to abide by their little agreement.

I spoke to the detectives about the voice stress test, and they were sure he was guilty; the test said so. Something about the man's confession of his sexual arrangement with the victim's mother made more sense to me.

I brought her in, and in thirty minutes she admitted she'd lied about the whole thing and was actually just mad at the maintenance man for not keeping his part of the bargain.

I advised the detectives about her confession and they still said, "He must have done something else we don't know about; the test says he was lying, so he's lying." I shook my head and left the room. No machine can measure a person's ability to lie.

This is the kind of gauntlet that the police recruit has to complete to make it through the hiring process—and you'd think it would work, wouldn't you? Surely no bad seeds could make it through this kind of process.

Casey Davis had a goal to become a cop from the time he was a kid. He made it through the gauntlet and was hired as a police officer in a large department. He was a single guy living large. He was a cop in the city he was raised in, and was wearing the uniform, badge and gun while walking in the same neighborhoods he had walked as a child just a few short years earlier.

He was hired at the age of twenty-three. He paid his dues on the street, and very soon was rewarded with a position making a difference in the city's school districts, working as a school resource officer (SRO). Davis had always felt he had a special knack for working with kids, especially kids who were at risk in the inner city.

He couldn't wait to jump into the SRO position and start making a difference. He applied himself to the position, volunteering to participate in the department's police explorer program (a kind of junior police officer volunteer program) and police athletic league as well. Davis felt that if he could make a difference to the kids, and help make a change for the better in where kids ended up, then he was going to do everything he could to make sure that happened.

Davis worked quietly at the position, teaching kids about the reality of drugs and how to make good choices. Davis made a serious attempt to win over the teachers and administrators in his schools. Previous cops assigned to the school had been older, gnarly, battle-worn veteran cops. They could be prickly and, frankly, kind of scary to the educators. Davis had replaced one of them in this assignment, and planned to make the most of his more polished and socially acceptable mannerisms.

In a few short months, he had proven to be a welcome change from his older predecessor. The school administrators could not have been more pleased with this smiling and less-frightening addition to their faculty.

In his off-duty time, Davis would often be found attending sporting events the kids were involved in and mentoring young volunteer explorer cadets in the city's explorer program.

All good things must come to an end, however.

Times were tough after the latest economic downturn, and the police department had to make deep cuts in its budget. The SRO program was cut, and Davis was sent back to patrol. He still maintained his presence in the explorer and police athletic programs, however, and volunteered as much as he could in the city's school district during his time off. He intended to keep his hard-won relationships with the school district personnel relevant.

Cynical veterans would shake their heads at his enthusiasm for working with the city's at-risk kids. They felt it was not normal for a guy to become a cop and want to work with kids so quickly. Cops are hired to crunch crime and battle bad guys, getting down and dirty in the streets and learning the ropes of the court system. Davis had spent minimal time on the streets, and the old-timers felt it in their guts that something was different about the guy. No polygraph or psych exam could identify what they tried to explain to each other over coffee. The guy just "felt wrong."

Granted, if he had spent more time on the streets, and had paid more dues, they would have been more comfortable with his time spent with kids. Often, veteran cops feel the need to give back to the younger generation after spending their time in the streets; veteran cops thus often end up in the schools trying to teach at-risk kids how to rise above their conditions and make better choices. Young cops rarely end up there so quickly. Cops like Davis who were not yet hardened by the streets and still proudly wore their baby fat just set off the alarms in the old timers' heads.

About a year passed after the department had to cut the SRO program, and Davis was still working as diligently as ever in his off time with the Police Athletic League and the explorer program.

The department had cut deep into many of its programs, but one program that had not been cut was the Internet crimes unit. The ICU investigates cases of people committing fraud online and advertising for prostitutes in online forums. This particular area of investigations is growing incredibly. Davis had shown no interest in the ICU. The unit, however, knew about him, and in the spring of that year had enough information to obtain a warrant to seize and search his home computer. They arrested Davis for attempting to purchase child pornography on the Internet.

The police department administration issued a press release stating that, as far as they knew, Davis's illegal activities had not spread into the schools, and they had no report of Davis abusing any of the children either there or in the Police Athletic League or explorer program.

This was, frankly, a pipe dream. Pedophiles work their whole lives to gain the kind of access to children that Davis had achieved. There was no way he hadn't abused any of the children he had "mentored" while in such a position of trust in the schools.

As is invariably the case when a break comes in a case like this one, children who had been too ashamed to talk to their parents finally decided to come forward. After a few more months of investigation, Davis was charged with nearly 200 counts of sexual abuse of the children he so loudly professed to wanting to protect and mentor.

He had come up with all kinds of clever ruses to manipulate the kids. The one that was best-known to the public was a story that Davis had concocted about a very contagious fungus spreading through the locker rooms of the teams he mentored and coached. He had the kids strip, and then would physically "inspect" them for the virus.

After a more extensive search of his computer was conducted, a video was found that Davis had made of himself abusing several young boys. He apparently watched it repeatedly to relive the events. He was a very sick man.

Davis was thirty years old when his twisted house of cards fell apart and he was criminally charged. He'd made himself out to be a hero in the eyes of the people who worked with kids in the inner city. He fooled teachers, administrators, coaches, and even a lot of cops.

In the end, though, the suspicions the older veterans had voiced about him proved to be true. He just did not "feel right." No polygraph test, voice stress analysis, or psychological exam had caught this bad seed. He had clearly walked through the gauntlet untouched, and worked as a wolf walking among the sheep.

The veteran cops knew what the tests could never understand. There is no test to show what makes a good cop. Davis received what amounted to a life sentence for the sexual abuse he had inflicted on the children.

Davis rose to hero status quickly, showing that the pre-employment tests were worthless. Fortunately he was caught, and dived right back down to zero.

CHAPTER SIXTEEN

GREG JOHNSON

POLITICS IS ONE THING THAT you never want to involve yourself in as a cop. The politics that can exist at a city or county level can be unbelievably brutal. Greg Johnson found that out the hard way. Johnson applied for a job with the local police department and made the cut. He somehow made it through the gauntlet of psychological tests, polygraphs, voice stress analyses, and background checks. He then passed the physical fitness exam with an almost perfect score. He was physically fit, smart, and eager to make a difference. He graduated from the state police academy and started working the midnight shift after successfully passing his four-month field-training phase.

Johnson was still on probation, as police departments have learned that even passing a battery of tests is not a guarantee that the new hire will work out. Most departments have at least a year of probation that must also be passed for the new recruit finally to be accepted as a full-time police officer. Johnson passed his year-long probation successfully, without a hitch. Nothing had popped up to show that anything was suspicious about the man.

The latest round of elections had begun to heat up in the city. The mayor was running for reelection, and had made a lot of enemies in the police department during his previous two terms. His decisions were based on his priorities, not the priorities of the police department, and a lot of times that placed him in a position that was seen as opposing that of the cops.

Johnson had been a cop long enough now to know that the mayor's continued occupation of his office meant more cuts for the police department and lower pay for the officers. Like most cops, he hated to sit back and watch while the world passed him by. Just complaining about a problem was worthless.

So Johnson decided to act. He started to support the mayor's opponent in the election quite vocally, and actively campaigned for him. Johnson became more and more involved in the city's politics, and eventually even caught the mayor's attention. Johnson did this by making up a billboard attacking the current mayor, attaching it to his minivan, and having his wife drive the van through the city. The mayor saw the van and wrote down the license plate.

The mayor then called his buddy, the chief of police, and had him find out who was driving this mobile billboard through the city. The chief had the license plate checked out and found out the vehicle belonged to one of his own officers. He was upset, to say the least. The chief had his own political aspirations, and he was not about to have them derailed by Johnson.

The mayor asked the chief to take care of the problem. At first he just called the officer in and tried in a subtle way to intimidate him. That had always worked in the past. Having the chief, who had married into one of the more politically powerful families in the city, as an enemy was not a good idea for a young cop.

Most cops the chief tried to intimidate backed down. Johnson didn't; he doubled his efforts in campaigning against the sitting mayor, in effect challenging the chief and mayor to try to stop him from doing so. Johnson had no idea just how far the men would go to smear his name. Like most people, he judged others by his own value system, and it would never have occurred to him to lie or mislead others about anything. He campaigned honestly and straightforwardly for his candidate.

About two weeks had passed since the meeting with the chief, and suddenly Johnson found himself in the middle of a nasty internal investigation. It was highly publicized in the local press that he had been accused of stealing a man's wallet while on duty.

The chief was clearly and very publically disturbed at the thought that one of his officers could be a thief. After all, this officer had passed all the background tests and had been working the streets for some time. The chief promised in a press release to get to the bottom of this situation and make sure that if Johnson were found to be a thief, he would be punished.

Johnson had a rude awakening to the realities of the city's politics. Right and wrong don't apply in the political world. The line around what is real becomes very grey when powerful people in a city get involved. They don't live by the same standards and are not above tactical press releases and baseless accusations to destroy anyone who dares to get in their way.

Johnson found this out the hard way. At first he fought back and tried to give the chief and the mayor a taste of their own medicine. He knew that the chief had accessed the motor vehicle records that identified his license number illegally; only cops working a criminal investigation could access them. The chief deftly sidestepped this accusation, and it also fell onto deaf ears in the press corps. No one wanted to challenge the powerfully placed chief of police. Johnson continued to take a beating in the easily manipulated press.

The reality is that nothing was ever proven against Johnson. He was never decertified by the state, and no criminal charges were ever brought against him for theft. The message he received, however, was loud and clear: *Keep up this political campaigning, and you will find your life and career destroyed.*

Johnson could not believe what was happening. He fought the good fight and did the best he could, but he was no match for the unscrupulous power brokers of the city.

Eventually he resigned from the police department and took a job working as a contractor for a security firm. It was not police work, and he no longer felt he was making a difference. He was lost and disillusioned by the experience.

Good cops are very much living in a dream world at times. They believe in what they think is right. They believe that you have to try to make a difference and be part of the solution, not the problem. Johnson had found out the hard way that the good guys don't always win. It shook his world.

He started to bounce from job to job, trying to find the purpose he had felt as a cop. He was never able to find it. His wife divorced him, and he moved away to a smaller city to try to start over. He was a good father, and took care of his kids after his divorce, making sure to spend time with them whenever he could.

But one night, depressed and feeling overwhelmed at the turn of events that had seemingly destroyed his life, Johnson started drinking. He was pretty drunk when he decided to get into his car and try to go see a girl he had recently met through some friends. He'd driven maybe a mile when the state trooper saw him weaving in and out of his lane. The trooper stopped Johnson and, after performing the necessary sobriety tests, charged him with DUI.

Johnson could not believe his bad luck. Less than two years earlier, he had been a sworn police officer, proudly wearing the uniform. Now he was sitting in the very jail into which he himself had booked criminals. How could this be real?

Johnson got out of jail the next morning and tried to figure out what to do. He still hoped to get back into law enforcement, but if he were convicted of the DUI he would never get hired. His future would have to lie in another career field. Johnson was desperate. He had to find a way out of this.

Johnson had a friend who worked in one of the smaller police departments in the area. He called him and asked him if he had any suggestions. Was there anything that he could think of that Johnson could do to salvage this?

The ex-cop and current cop talked things over and came up with a plan. They decided to contact the trooper and try to convince him to drop the charges. The plan was a poor one, and in retrospect, you have to wonder what the hell they were thinking. Regardless, they did contact the trooper, and over a series of meetings offered him a couple of thousand dollars to drop the charges.

He wasn't about to drop the charges. Soon Johnson was back in the press—front page, as a matter of fact. The article described him as the former police officer who had been accused of stealing a man's wallet, and who was now charged with trying to bribe a state trooper to drop pending DUI charges.

Johnson had really dug himself a hole. He ended up pleading to the charges; the police officer he had asked to help him was also charged. That cop also lost his job and was found guilty of the bribery attempt.

CHAPTER SEVENTEEN
TIM NELSON

TIM NELSON WAS SEVENTEEN WHEN he went into the army. He was trained as an infantryman and then went on to Vietnam. It was late in the war and he would spend about a year there, and was later shipped home to complete his enlistment. He came back to his home state after his army hitch and bounced from job to job until he ended up testing to become a state trooper. He passed the tests, and found he liked the independence the job provided. He excelled as a trooper. This was when I met him. He was at the tail end of his career, and I was at the beginning of mine. I was a deputy sheriff, and we would frequently go for coffee together during the long night shifts.

Tim was a solid guy. Those of us in the sheriff's department felt that the troopers were not real cops like us. They specialized only handling traffic cases, and were completely out of their element if they showed up to help out at a family fight, or worse, a brawl at one of the bars that dotted the county. Tim was an exception to that rule. The time he had spent in Vietnam and since, working in various contracting jobs, had seasoned him. He could hold his own in any situation, and we frequently appreciated his arrival on a scene. At least he did no harm, and more often than not he helped us out. He was a pretty big guy, standing 6'3", and he was fairly fit.

One night the fellas at the local country bar decided they didn't like the way a group of hippies (yeah, seriously—they said "hippies") was looking at them. One thing led to another, and a huge fight broke out.

Every available car was called and responded to the fight. We had our hands full trying to get the scene under control. There were just too many combatants and not enough of us.

Tim showed up and started to do what very few troopers would ever do, at least while I was a cop. He waded into the fight and started throwing people out. Literally—he physically grabbed them and threw them out. Anyone who tried to fight back found out fast that Tim might be older, but he was still able to scrap with the best of them. Like I said, he was a solid guy, capable in almost every way.

After the fight was over, we all met up for a quick drink and started to write reports, laughing and reliving the battle we had just survived. That was the reality of bar fights. It came down to survival, and we all knew it.

Things went on like this for some time. Tim liked to work the late shift, and so did most of us. We'd meet up at the closest 24-hour convenience store and talk about the night's events over a drink or coffee. If there was ever a hint that anything was wrong, this might have been where it was first evident.

There was one moment I remember a look in his eye when a beautiful young woman walked into the store. She had obviously just left the nearby bar and was dressed to kill. He eyed her carefully, almost like a predator.

He then said, "I guess she isn't drunk, we'll let her drive home." That was it. It wasn't the things he said; it was the look in his eye. Momentarily, he looked evil and predatory.

About nine or ten months later, I showed up for coffee at the usual time, and Tim was not there. I asked around, and no one knew where he was. It was very much a "do not ask" response I received. Finally I went to the information source that all cops go to when they want to know what the hell is going on: dispatchers.

They told me that the solid, down-to-earth Tim Nelson had been stopping drivers for speeding on a nearby interstate late at night. If they were men, he wrote a ticket and sent then on their way. If they were women, he would stress that they were likely to get a very expensive ticket for their reckless speeding. The ticket would cost several hundred dollars, and then their insurance would go up as well. This was likely to cost them a lot of money overall. Almost without exception the women would say, "Isn't there some way to make this go away?" Crying, they did not realize the door that they had just opened.

Nelson would continue to emphasize the cost and the hardship the women had just caused their families, and when he felt he had them right where he wanted them, he would soften his hard-line attitude just a bit.

Maybe there was a way they could come to some kind of agreement. Apparently this worked for some time. Nelson would make the offer of "working out a deal"—a blowjob in exchange for dropping the ticket. Surprisingly, some women apparently did follow through with the deal.

Nelson continued to stop speeders and make deals where he could. He was finally caught when he stopped a car that he had stopped before. He recognized the woman as a previous speeder who had "made a deal." This time, the woman had a female friend with her.

Nelson felt comfortable making his pitch in a more blatant, in-your-face manner than usual. But the woman had a witness this time, and refused to "deal" the ticket away.

Nelson had made a big mistake. The next morning, the woman was in the section commander's office with her witness, filing her complaint.

Nelson was relieved of duty, and eventually made a plea deal with prosecutors. He resigned as a state trooper and moved on to another career. We were all shocked, because there was no hint of this behavior in anything we saw—except, as I mentioned, that one day and that predatory look.

CHAPTER EIGHTEEN

LARRY MORAVEC

LARRY MORAVEC GREW UP IN a rural part of the county. Every day he would board the bus and begin the long ride to the schools he attended. Every day the bus passed the house of a deputy sheriff whom Larry idolized. He would frequently daydream about what it would be like to be a deputy and patrol the entire county.

As Larry grew older, he noticed the different cars that the deputy would use for work. First, a patrol car—a police package cruiser decked out with light bar, sirens, spotlights, and a fresh, clean paint job. He could see the shotgun rack holding a tactical shotgun, and extra antennas on the trunk and behind the light bar. The car looked awesome, and he imagined himself as the driver heading to a robbery in progress, headed out to make a difference. Later, the deputy had a K-9 truck, and, much later, the unmarked vehicle of an administrator. Larry knew one thing from the time he was a little boy: he wanted to know what it would be like to make a difference and be like that deputy.

Larry graduated high school in the middle of his class. He was one of those guys who had a natural knack for blending in. Everyone liked him, for the most part, and yet when you asked them his name, no one could remember it. In high school, this made him feel disliked or perhaps just tolerated by his peers. No one could seem to remember Larry, and yet he had a gift for making people trust him immediately. That gift would turn out to be an amazing asset.

Larry later said that his parents had raised him always to be direct and honest. They emphasized strongly to him, "When you have a problem, confront it head on—don't hide from it and just hope it will go away." Larry took that advice to heart, and it served him well for most of his life.

One day Larry was talking to a guy he had just met at a family party. The man asked him what he planned to do with his life now that he had graduated high school. Larry expressed his lifelong desire to be a cop. He was still too young actually to become a cop, but he was an adult, and could do other things in the field. The guy listened more intently than perhaps Larry realized. Larry did not know it, but the stranger was actually an undercover narcotics officer.

He sized Larry up and watched how well he communicated with other people at the party. He quickly noticed Larry had an amazing gift with people. They were instantly put at ease with his genuine manner and his habit of being direct and honest.

A couple of days later, the undercover cop contacted Larry and asked him if he was serious about the comment he'd made about wanting to be a cop. Larry replied he was, but he was not yet twenty-one and he would have to wait a few more years before he could even apply for any cop job.

The narcotics officer offered him the chance to act as a CI, or confidential informant. He would go undercover, acting as a police agent, and infiltrate local drug rings. Larry would be given an alias and wear a wire. He would make undercover buys as the agent directed him.

It was an opportunity that would scare the hell out of most people. Larry thought it over for about a second-and-a-half and said, "Sure, I'm in—when do we start?" The veteran officer smiled; he knew that Larry would be a one-in-a-million CI.

Larry became "Bill,"—and Bill racked up an unbelievable number of arrests for the narcotics strike force. He had a gift for always being in the right place at the right time.

A few years passed, and Larry was old enough now to enter law enforcement through the front door. He applied and was accepted as a correctional officer by his local sheriff's department.

He started working his way up the food chain as soon as he arrived, paying his dues in the jail, working shitty assignments without complaining. Soon he was out on the road, driving that patrol car he had dreamed about every day as a young boy. It was his dream come true.

He was finally where he wanted to be. He was married to a beautiful young woman and had the job and the life he had dreamed of. He bought a house and started to build his version of the American dream. One night while Larry was at work, a friend called him. The friend sounded a little weird, and so Larry, being direct as he always was, asked, "What's wrong?"

The friend paused; he didn't know how to tell Larry what he had noticed on his way home from work. The friend was a cop too, and lived in the same neighborhood as Larry.

On his way home, as he turned the corner onto the street they both lived on, the friend thought he saw the garage door at Larry's house closing, and he thought he saw a police car in the garage. Larry was a deputy sheriff, and the car his friend saw was clearly a regular police car.

Larry loved his wife, and she loved him. They had been married barely long enough to be out of the honeymoon phase. He thought it over and decided his friend was playing a mean prank on him, so he blew it off.

When Larry came home that morning, he looked around the house and found nothing out of place. His wife greeted him like always, and they talked about his night. Larry watched her carefully and later admitted that he noticed a distance between them—something in the way she looked away that was barely noticeable, and yet definitely there.

A couple of nights passed, and again Larry's cop friend called and told him, "Hey, man, I am *not* kidding—there's a fucking cop car in your garage. I parked a ways off and watched as the car pulled in and the garage door closed."

Larry said, "Thanks. I'll look into it."

Every cop has been on these calls. You feel for the people who are betrayed, you feel their hurt and loss. You just pray it never happens to you. Larry thought it over. He had to see with his own eyes what the hell was going on at his home when he had gone to work.

He asked his sergeant if he could leave the area to which he was assigned to make a quick trip home. He told his sergeant that his wife had been very sick and that he had tried to call her and couldn't reach her. He just wanted to check and make sure that she was alright, and would be right back. The calls were slow that night, so the sergeant gave him the okay to head home. Larry said thanks, and was on his way.

He really hoped that he would arrive at the house and find out that his friend had been playing a prank, but in his gut, he remembered the distance in his wife's eyes and the change in how it felt when she hugged him in the morning, when he arrived home after work.

The drive home was usually very long when he came home in the mornings, tired and ready to go to sleep. Tonight, however, the drive was over faster than he realized. He arrived in his neighborhood and parked a couple of houses away from his own. Cop tactics were kicking in.

He got out of the car and then thought it over. He went back and took off his gun belt and put it in the trunk. He really hoped that he wouldn't find his wife with another man, but if he did, he didn't want to leave himself the opportunity to make a bad situation much worse.

Larry snuck into his own house, quietly slipping down the hall to the master bedroom, and peered through the crack in the door. His heart sank in his chest and he felt sick. There was his beautiful bride, naked and asleep with a man Larry had formerly thought of as a friend.

A fellow cop had been fucking his wife and now they were both asleep in Larry's house and in Larry's bed. Larry said that he didn't remember how long he sat there staring at the scene in disbelief.

Sometimes it's like that on a crime scene as well: you get out and look at it and your mind finds that it is just too horrible to grasp. It takes you time to process it and understand what you are seeing. Your mind shuts down for a minute, time stops, and you stare, trying to make what you are seeing fit into your world, the world you left just moments ago. That world is now torn away and reality stares back, unblinking and brutal.

Larry said he remembered entering the room and grabbing the former friend and fellow cop. He picked him up off the bed and began to give the man the beating of his life. He said he didn't remember hearing his wife screaming at him, and barely felt her slaps and punches while she tried to defend her lover.

Larry was hell-bent on making sure this motherfucker never forgot the night he was caught in bed with Larry's wife. Larry said he didn't remember when the cops pulled up to his house. He thinks his wife must have called 911, but he isn't sure. All he remembered was pounding the naked cop's head into the cement outside the house over and over, and yelling at him, "What now, bitch?"

Larry was still in shock moments later when another cop grabbed him and pulled him off of the bloody and naked pile of shit. He had no idea that it was a cop who had grabbed him, and he punched the cop in the face, knocking him on his ass. A few moments later, several cops grabbed him and restrained him. Paramedics were called for the wounded naked man Larry had beaten into submission.

Reality hit Larry hard. He was put on administrative leave for two weeks. The ex-friend Larry caught in bed with his wife was put on administrative leave as well, but for only two days. He was back at work and basically given a reprimand, a slight slap on the wrist, and told not to do that again, bad boy (wink, wink).

The other cop was married as well, and had a newborn baby girl waiting at home. Apparently that didn't matter to him either. He left his wife and young child.

Larry was brought back after his administrative leave and investigation and told by his chief, "You would have been better off killing the son of a bitch." He was then fired on the spot and walked to the front door of the police department. Larry's entire life went to shit in very short order.

However, the story isn't over yet—not by a long shot. The piece-of-shit cop Larry caught in his house got a call one night from his estranged wife. She was a dispatcher for the local police department. The whispers in the hallways at work, the shame and the grief, had been too much. She had been drinking heavily and wanted him to come home and work things out. She said they had a child together and they needed to put her needs first. The devastated and drunk wife said to her cheating husband, "Come home now, or I'll kill myself."

His reply? "Don't talk about it, bitch. Do it."

So she did, shooting herself in the head and ending the misery he'd caused.

Even more fucked up than this is that the cheating cop married Larry's cheating wife and told his daughter that his new wife was her real mother. To this day, the child has no idea her real mother died the way she did, or why.

Larry fell long and hard himself. He quickly fell into a drunken stupor, and then rekindled his old contacts in the narcotics world. In no time at all he was knee-deep in alcohol and cocaine, perhaps making his own attempt at suicide. He said that he was in a very dark place. Sitting at home alone, watching recordings of his wedding day over and over, getting drunk and staying as high as he could.

Looking back now, Larry said he realizes he would have continued on that way till he died. However, a close friend came over to the house and went medieval on his ass. He pulled down all of the old wedding pictures Larry had left on the walls, grabbed the recordings of the wedding, and threw them all away.

The friend said "This shit ends right here, right now! You got fucked over, it's true, but it is time to man up and deal with it." He was in Larry's face, screaming at him trying to wake him up.

Larry said that one moment saved his life. He would never again be a cop, but he realized he could survive this. He decided to try to repair his shattered life and move on.

Reality can be incredibly brutal. Larry fell hard and barely survived the betrayal of his wife and her fucked-up lover.

CHAPTER NINETEEN
RANDI GIBBS

SOMETIMES YOU NEVER REALLY KNOW who you are working with, or for that matter, sleeping with. Chad Hansen was a reserve officer with the sheriff's department. He had wanted to be a deputy sheriff for as long as he could remember. He had tested for the job and scored low. He just could not seem to get the subtle ins and outs of what it took to be a cop. Still, he didn't give up. He volunteered in his off time as a reserve officer, and listened to every deputy he rode with. He asked a lot of questions and tried to understand why the officers did what they did. He noticed that each one had a different style, different method of doing things, and he hoped to learn from them. During the day he was a sheet-metal worker, and at night a reserve deputy. It took him several years, but eventually he did get hired, and in no time at all he was out on the road, handling calls and living his dream.

After Chad was hired as a deputy, he had more confidence and felt better about himself. It had been a long and hard effort to get through the hiring process, but he had finally made it. He saw everything in his life as an obstacle to overcome—a challenge to be accepted and then defeated.

One of Chad's passions was weightlifting, and in particular body-building. He ate a very strict diet and knew exactly how many grams of protein, carbohydrates, and fats he ate. He was obsessed with his diet and working out. His obsession paid off, and he had an amazing physique. He was a small guy, maybe 5'6," but he was powerfully built, and weighed nearly 190 lbs. He was very proud of the body that he had built, and had his uniforms tailored to show off his muscular physique.

One day while working out in the gym, Chad noticed a female bodybuilder. She'd been coming in regularly, and they started to talk about programs, strict diets, and their goals. Chad introduced himself, and said that he worked for the sheriff's department.

The female bodybuilder was instantly interested in him. She asked all kinds of questions about the process to get hired as a cop and what it took to do the job. She introduced herself as Randi Gibbs and told him that she, too, wanted to work in law enforcement.

Chad and Randi decided to meet after their workouts and started to go out to eat at a health food restaurant they both often frequented. They had a lot in common, and immediately hit it off.

Chad could not believe his good fortune. He was in the job he loved, and now had a girlfriend who was interested in the same hobbies and lifestyle. This was a huge change from his recently dissolved marriage. His previous wife was not into fitness, hated cops, and had recently become addicted to meth. He knew he had to end that relationship to make his life's goals a reality. Now it seemed to Chad like everything was finally falling into place.

Chad and Randi decided to move into an apartment together. At first it was just to share expenses. Randi had recently gone through a divorce as well, and had no desire to get back into another relationship. Chad was cool with that. He just liked having her around. He liked taking care of her, and had suggested that she apply at the sheriff's department the next time they had openings. He would let her go out as a ride along with him so that she could see what it was like to be a deputy sheriff.

Chad really liked helping Randi and taking care of her. In their relationship, he was the caregiver, and she was more detached and aloof—not talking much, and keeping Chad at a distance. Chad, as usual, took this a challenge, and pursued her even more diligently. Eventually she decided she had nothing to lose, and they actually started dating and sleeping together.

Everyone at work knew when this occurred, because Chad was so proud that he had landed this amazingly beautiful woman that he could not stop bragging about her. Every single day we heard about Randi this and Randi that…blah, blah, blah.

When he started bragging about their sex life, however, we all stopped and listened.

Chad said he was surprised when she totally took over that aspect of the relationship. He did what she wanted and when. He described her as fierce and demanding, and said that at first he was a little intimidated by her. I have to admit we were all envious when he said she had an almost daily habit of taking his handcuffs out and securing him to their bed before she fucked his brains out. He said she was incredibly fit, and would leave him bruised and worn out before she was done with him. We all stared into space as we tried to imagine this. Randi was hot as hell, and we envied the muscle-bound deputy.

Randi was eventually able to secure a position at the jail as a correctional officer. She was strong and fit, and not the least bit intimidated by any of the inmates. Often when a call went out for help from another officer in a fight with an inmate, she would be the first to respond and engage the inmate, soundly kicking his ass. She was as proud of her physicality as Chad was of his.

They both worked out with an intensity that few of us could match, each of them lifting and working out after work, and eating a diet most of us would gag on. The health food was not tasty, but it did have some amazing results. They were very fit.

Chad made a point of bragging even louder about how much more sexually dominant Randi had become since she was working in the jail. He said that after being in a fight, she would be especially demanding. One time he even took off his shirt and body armor to show us the bruises on his chest and shoulders from her knees as she rode him. He was quite proud, and we were all very envious. At least for a while.

Roy Calhoon was a mean and nasty guy when he was sober. When he was drinking, no one wanted to be around him. One night, Roy Calhoon was higher than usual. He had been drinking heavily all day and had scored some cocaine from a friend of his. He was feeling pretty good before the cocaine; after he snorted it, he said he didn't remember much of what happened.

What he didn't remember was that he went on a spree of breaking into houses and apartments and tried to rape two women. One was able to escape, and called the police. The second woman wasn't able to escape.

Roy raped her repeatedly and brutally. He beat her up badly and spent several hours torturing her sexually. Eventually she, too, escaped after he passed out, and she called the police. She was a bloody mess when the police arrived.

The previous victim was able to identify him as her attacker as well. Roy was arrested and charged with both incidents. Roy was booked into jail and was looking at a long stay in both the county jail and the state prison for aggravated rape.

He said he had no memory of the incident, but his apprehension at the scene of the second rape, covered in the victim's blood, left no doubts as to his guilt. He was booked into our jail by the arresting officers.

Roy's trial took some time, and he was in jail for about sixteen months before he was actually convicted and sent to prison for the rapes. Most sexual offenders find jail not a lot of fun. The other inmates don't like sexual offenders, and neither do the correctional officers. But Roy had a different experience from most.

One night Randi was assigned to work the POD that housed the high-risk inmates. She relished the position she had over these men. They were dangerous because of the crimes they had committed, and yet here she was, a woman, in charge of them, watching over them and making them toe the line and do exactly as she demanded.

When Roy Calhoon arrived on the POD, he refused to show her any respect. He had had issues with women before the rapes, and he wasn't about to be told what to do by a female correctional officer. The two had a battle of wills, making a very public display of their instant dislike and hatred of each other.

Randi would task Roy with shitty chores that he hated to do, and force him to do each of the tasks to her exact requirements. The other inmates stayed out of the way; none of them wanted to experience her wrath. They all had the idea it was better to keep on her good side than piss her off.

Frequently Randi would come to the floor late at night and get Roy up, handcuffing and putting leg irons on him. She would grab him by the hair and talk shit, taunting him about what a big man he was for raping those women. Did he feel so big now? Probably not. Then Randi would walk him out to do some chore. Roy would return about an hour or so later, silent and humiliated. The other inmates didn't want to be in his shoes.

Randi would brag to Chad about how she would bully the inmates, specifically Roy, detailing the menial tasks he would have to perform and how she purposely humiliated him every chance she got. Chad was a little frightened by how aggressive she was in her descriptions, but never voiced his fear to her. Always, after each story she told him, after a long night at work, she would handcuff him to their bed, force him to go down on her, and then they would have intercourse.

It was always the same, very physical and very aggressive. Chad was in heaven. He would detail each morning tryst to us every night at work.

One night, Chad's world came falling down. He came home from work, and there was Randi. She had been relieved of duty at the jail pending an investigation. Chad felt sure that she had finally gone too far while intimidating one of the inmates. He was proud of how scrappy she was, and while she might be punished or reprimanded, he felt sure that she wouldn't lose her job.

Randi was not so sure. She started to detail the events that had happened that night. Randi had been removing Roy Calhoon from the POD of high-risk offenders on a regular basis, and she would usually describe to Chad most of what would happen—but not all of it. What she had not described she now went into in great detail, while she glared into his eyes defiantly.

Unashamed, she told Chad how she would force Roy to do some tasks, and then take him to a large utility closet. There, she would strip off his pants and force him to have sex with her. She would lock the closet and strip off her uniform, forcing Roy to fuck her. She said she wanted him to know what it felt like to be powerless and to be forced into sex by a stronger, more physically dominant person—in this case, a female.

Chad was sick to his stomach. He knew that Randi was aggressive sexually, but he never imagined she would fuck someone else while they were together, much less a violent rapist and an inmate. He was devastated. Then she dropped the real bomb on him.

Still glaring at him, she started to recall each morning after work. Smiling, she said, "You had to know this was going on. Each morning I would come home and tell you about how I humiliated him. You would laugh and think it was funny, remember? Then I would handcuff you to our bed with your own handcuffs and force you to clean his cum off of me."

Chad lost his mind. He went into the bathroom of their apartment and threw up. All those instances he had bragged about to the guys at work suddenly now became a nightmare. He had had no idea what had been going on while they had been living together. Randi had secretly been humiliating both him and the inmate.

Chad's world came crashing down. He moved out of the apartment that day and hoped that no one would find out what Randi had done to him. Unfortunately for Chad, we all knew what had happened, and why, within 24 hours of Randi being told to go home from work. Apparently, Roy was one of several inmates she was forcing to have sex with her. One of the other guys became jealous of her and Roy Calhoon, and turned her in to the other correctional officers.

Randi lost her job in the jail, and the two deputies ended their relationship instantly. Randi was never criminally charged, and quietly disappeared. We never mentioned Randi's name to Chad again, each of us hoping when we went home that nothing like this would ever happen to us.

Chad eventually dated again and reclaimed his shattered life. He never ever bragged again about his girlfriend and their sexual exploits, however.

The reality is that you never really know who you are working with, or sleeping with.

CHAPTER TWENTY

JOHNNY HEYWOOD

JOHNNY HEYWOOD WAS A SENIOR in college a year before the terrorist attacks occurred on 9/11/2001. Heywood had already decided to become an officer in the military and had already completed the necessary paperwork well before the incident occurred. When the planes came crashing into the twin towers, Heywood had already decided to become an officer and was headed into a special operations unit.

Heywood was a gifted athlete, and as mentally tough as any officer in special operations. Heywood was distinguished in several different and classified operations, and when the time came, Heywood elected to get out of the military and become a cop. Heywood landed in our department, and to be honest, at first I wasn't impressed. Heywood seemed a little too friendly to be a cop, and I was frankly suspicious of the whole call-to-duty-in-Afghanistan story we'd all heard.

Heywood made friends quickly with the new bunch of cops the chief had recently hired, and quickly fell in with the group, accepted as one of their own. In some ways, I was envious. Social settings and work relationships were never easy for me. To see a new officer be accepted so easily was a wake-up call regarding how alienated I really was.

The department had a golf team, and Heywood quickly became the star. Heywood attended college on a golf scholarship and had excelled at it. Not only had Heywood been a 4.0 GPA student, but apparently a gifted athlete as well. Could life be that perfect for anyone? Apparently it could for some people.

Heywood and I rarely worked the same shift, but when we did, I remained as scarce as possible. I would arrive as a backup and keep quiet. Listening to Heywood turn on the charm, working the magic on the people in the inner city, was alarming. We had totally different styles of communication.

One day we finally ended up on a call that totally went to shit. It was a large brawl of drunken Cinco de Mayo celebrators, none of whom had any family even remotely connected to Mexico. That never mattered, however; any reason to drink was a good reason for most people in the inner city.

When we arrived, the fight was in full swing. Nothing we could do but wade in and start removing people from the mix. I found a new respect for Heywood that day, Heywood might have been smaller than the rest of us, and on a golf scholarship in college, but damn, Heywood could fight. Jesus, it was amazing. Some people just have a gift for scrapping. I don't know why or where they develop it, but it seems to come naturally to them, and fighting definitely came naturally to Heywood. The normally smiling and polite Heywood displayed an incredible gift at taking much larger and apparently stronger opponents apart in no time. I admit I was impressed.

A few months later, Heywood was transferred to narcotics. Undercover work came as naturally to Heywood as golf and fighting. Again, I was envious. I never did understand narcotics. In the gang world, I was almost frighteningly comfortable; in narcotics, I was lost. Heywood took to it immediately. It was another gift.

Heywood got married a short time after entering the narcotics strike force. I wasn't invited to the wedding, but I heard that she had picked a real loser as a husband. I guess even the women in our field have issues, and end up with mates for whom they are the worst possible match. Heywood was no exception to that rule. Regardless, Heywood was joyfully married, and moved into a new home with her tanned and attractive man.

She had a hard time making ends meet with the new high-maintenance husband, however. He was not exactly a hard worker, and he rarely had a job. He demanded a lot of attention and expected her to buy him expensive gifts, and often. I would guess he was a male version of a trophy wife—but while he may have been pleasing to her eye, he seemed a real loser to everyone else.

Eventually the trophy husband spent Heywood into so much debt she had to take a leave of absence from the police department. She had to go back to Afghanistan, this time as a civilian contractor.

Heywood had survived a lot of intense situations in the military in Afghanistan and did not really want to return. However, as a contractor, she could make four times the salary she made at the department. She talked it over with her trophy husband, and he agreed it would be a good idea.

Heywood filled out the paperwork and took a leave of absence from the department for a year. She set up a bank account in both her and her trophy husband's names. She had her paychecks deposited directly into the joint account, and her trophy man was supposed to pay off the bills and handle the finances while she was gone.

A couple of months later, Heywood was back in "the sandbox," as desert theatres of operation are called. She was conducting opium-interdiction operations for a private security company. She rode in convoys, battling drug lords and destroying large fields of poppies. She lived in B huts, plywood shacks housing six people each. She showered in community showers, wearing sandals to avoid the rampant disease they contained, and never touching the light switches, as many of her fellow contactors had been electrocuted by the faulty wiring in the temporary buildings. Danger was everywhere, and it was not uncommon that she would have to run for cover in the springtime when the Taliban shelled the air base at which she was housed.

This went on for a little over a year—Heywood working in war-torn Afghanistan and her husband paying off the bills back home. Leaving the trophy husband in charge of the money was the second real mistake that Heywood made in her life. The first was marrying the loser. While Heywood was in the sandbox working her ass off, getting shot at in firefights and gambling with her life against the Russian roulette of IEDs, her trophy husband was hitting the strip clubs, and eventually ended up with his own "trophy" mate.

She was a beauty with a black hole for a soul. They were made for each other. Heywood's husband told his soulless mate his situation, and they decided to take Heywood for every penny she could make.

The day finally arrived for Heywood to come home, and she was stoked. She had survived some really hairy situations: IEDs, firefights, convoy attacks—you name it, it happened. Yet somehow she had survived.

She told her trophy man when she was going to arrive, the flight, and time. She had missed him terribly; for some reason, she'd never seen him like the rest of us saw him. I guess the old saying that love is blind really must be true. She got off the plane really excited to see him.

He had told her that he had managed the money well, paid off the debt, and also paid off the mortgage on the house. He also told her that he loved her and missed her desperately. She imagined that in a week or two she would be back on the streets as a cop, debt-free, doing the job she loved, and sleeping with the man she loved.

After Heywood's plane landed, she walked up the enclosed tunnel and into the airport. Daydreaming, in her mind she saw her man running toward her and picking her up, happy to see her. Instead, there was a guy holding a sign with her name on it. Smiling, she imagined that a long black limousine would be waiting outside the terminal and that the man holding the sign would escort her to it, taking her to her trophy man, tanned and sexy, who would be waiting inside the car.

Still smiling, she walked up to the man and said, "Hi! I'm Johnny Heywood."

"Hello!" he responded. Then he said, "Sorry about this," and handed her a summons to appear in court.

Her trophy husband was divorcing her. This was her welcome home.

Heywood was shattered. She called some old friends from the police department, and they came to the airport to pick her up. When she arrived home, the house was empty. There was nothing there—no furniture, no dishes; even the appliances were gone.

It was only going to get worse for Heywood. She immediately went to the bank to close the joint account she'd held with her trophy man. When she arrived, she found the account was empty—it literally had a ZERO balance.

Not only was Heywood broke and her house empty, her trophy man had not paid the mortgage for several months, and their home was in foreclosure.

She went back to work at the police department. Everyone welcomed her back with smiles and hugs, but the welcome was short-lived. Heywood was incredibly tough, but this was just too much. The reality hit her hard, and she started to drink heavily, trying to cope. Her drinking quickly got out of control, and she was picked up for DUI just one month after she returned to work. A DUI is a career-ending charge for a cop.

Heywood not only lost her home and trophy husband, she lost her job—quickly traveling the bumpy road from hero to zero.

CHAPTER TWENTY-ONE

ALAN PREVOST

ALAN PREVOST WAS A COUPLE of years older than I was, and was hired at the city about a year before I was, as well. In the department, Prevost was known as a workaholic. He made it clear to every sergeant and shift supervisor that he was available for overtime shifts, at any time, day or night—it didn't matter.

Prevost lived for the almighty dollar. He was a great example of a cop who was addicted to the job and its salary. He chased overtime with such a vengeance that it became questionable whether it was safe for sergeants to use him to fill their shift openings. For example, in one 72-hour period, he worked 68 hours. Eventually they had to rein him in, because the city had an issue with the number of hours that he was on the job.

Perhaps I should really say that he was on the clock 68 hours. That would be more accurate. Prevost had a habit of cat-napping and working in areas that would allow him the opportunity to catch a few zzz's, as he put it, when the calls slowed down. The brass loved his supposed work ethic. The rest of us knew that he might be on the clock, but he wasn't working. He was slow to respond to calls, and did the bare minimum necessary to complete the call. There was no checking of details, no talking to suspects, and no looking into clues. He would arrive, record the facts and write the report, catch a nap, and then clear off to the next call. He saw no problem with this at all.

Alan was as committed to working part-time jobs as he was to working hours at the department. He would work security at rare coin and gem shows, movie set security, retail security, concerts. Any job you can imagine that would require a cop to be present, he would be working.

He was a force in motion when it came to "working." No one in the department worked more hours on the clock and accomplished less. He made an amazing amount of money sleeping in closets, corners, and dark parking lots, almost never going home except to shower and say hi to his kids, and then set back out in the quest for the almighty dollar.

He was able to "work" his way into a variety of units. He worked bike patrol, domestic violence crimes, gang task force, and even made it into the Community-Oriented Policing (COPs) unit. He never seemed to close any calls in any of the units by arrest, unless they fell into his lap and an arrest was impossible to avoid. The department didn't track actual convictions, so I have no idea what his conviction rate was, but I can imagine it was less-than-stellar.

Here is an example of his amazing work ethic: One night while working his usual overtime shifts, Prevost was called to a report of two men fighting on the west side of the city. He normally didn't work that area. The calmer, southeast side was his favorite area to work—fewer calls there, more naps. Tonight, though, he had to venture out and actually hit the west side. It was not exactly lily-white on the west side, and people often broke into fistfights and gang fights. Homicides weren't that infrequent there. A report came in that the two men were fighting, and had really been going at it for some time.

People on the west side didn't call police for a fight that amounted to a couple of punches; they only called to prevent someone from being killed, and even that was not a sure thing. Often we would get no reports from anyone that a fight had even occurred. The only way we knew that anything had happened at all was when people started showing up in the local emergency rooms with knife wounds or gunshot wounds. A car would pull up, drop off the bodies and drive away. Seriously, that was the way it was done. Dump the injured bodies and go.

Anyway, Prevost arrived on the west side and located the two combatants. They were on the verge of being homeless, and life had become brutally serious for each of them in the last couple of months. Each was poor, hungry, and literally fighting for survival. No one ever found out what they had been fighting about. They were both bloodied, and had beaten the hell out of each other.

Prevost did the usual bare minimum, asking them if they were okay. Did they need medical attention? Did anyone want to press charges? Because if they did, he would have to take them both to jail.

That was his standard approach: find a way to make the incident go away as quickly as possible. The less paperwork, the better—and back to the power nap.

The two men could not afford medical care, and neither wanted to be arrested. Each quickly agreed to leave the area immediately and go his own separate ways—no harm, no foul.

Prevost was happy with that solution, and minimized the seriousness of the fight. He claimed on the radio that neither combatant was seriously injured and that their disagreements had all been worked out. He was clear from the call.

Reality was very different. One of the combatants had been so severely beaten (which was painfully obvious at the scene) that he died the next day. He had severe internal injuries, and a bleeding hemorrhage on the brain. The mutual combat call had just become a potential homicide.

Detectives were called out. They investigated and discovered that Prevost had been assigned the call. Homicide detectives contacted Prevost to see if he had his notes from the incident.

It wasn't unreasonable for them to expect that he would at least get the men's names, dates of birth, physical descriptions, and addresses. The usual bare minimum a patrolman would obtain at a call requires at least checking for any warrants on the suspects, and that would require obtaining identification and making a positive ID of anyone involved in the call.

However, this was Prevost. That would require more effort than he put into 95 percent of his calls. He hadn't run the men to see if they were wanted for any previous crimes, and he hadn't asked for identification. He hadn't even asked them their names. He had absolutely nothing to show for his contact with the two men. Nothing.

The detectives were not only amazed, they were furious. At the time, Prevost had been a cop for fifteen years or more. He knew better, but just didn't care.

One of the detectives mentioned the case to me a few days later. He said that they considered charging Prevost for negligence, but that the department administration had squashed the idea. They didn't want the bad press. He asked me if that was standard for patrolmen now—not to take any information at a call. I laughed. Standard? No, not for most of us. For Prevost, though, it was normal.

The man died, and no charges were ever filed against anyone. About a week later, Prevost told me his version of the event. He was mad that the detectives had second-guessed him and questioned why he hadn't obtained either of the men's identification. He said, "Fuck them, they don't know what we do on the street. It is easy to second guess us when you're not out here in the battle."

I smiled. There would be no changing Prevost. He was never wrong, and saw himself as one of the hardest-working and most productive patrolman in the department.

Somehow, Prevost made it through his career and reached retirement. He continued to drain the department of resources and money by working shifts and details that popped up, while actually producing very little. We called it "sucking a check."

We compared the work ethic of cops like Alan Prevost and Mike Preston to that of prostitutes who would only give blowjobs. All did the bare minimum on the streets, yet they were all thought of as whores to the almighty dollar, willing to do anything for a buck.

Prevost loved to spend the money he made. It was part of his tremendous ego, making money and then spending it on stuff—stuff he would be sure to tell everyone that he'd purchased. Not that he could enjoy any of it; he was never home. But he did have it all, including tanning beds, laser-disc surround-sound theater systems, night-vision goggles, hand guns of every make and model, Caribbean cruises, motor homes, etc. He even had a home custom-built home with indoor and outdoor swimming pools and a hot tub. All of which he was rarely able to use, because he was a slave to the job.

Prevost thought very highly of himself, as you might have guessed. He thought that he deserved to be promoted and could not understand why he was never elevated up the food chain to sergeant or lieutenant. He knew that he belonged there, but in his mind the kiss-asses had banded together. He felt that they didn't want a cop who worked as hard as he saw himself working in their ranks, making them look bad. It has always amazed me how people rationalize and warp reality.

When the opportunity popped up at a smaller nearby department to apply for a recently-vacated chief's position, Prevost jumped at it. He had a resume that was impressive on paper. The reality was very different, but city councils have no idea of what makes a good cop, and even less of what makes a good chief. Prevost could schmooze the brass like nobody's business. He'd made a career out of making a molehill of effort look like a mountain of results. So the city council did what most city councils do, and hired the least-capable man for the job.

Prevost thought that he'd finally received his due as a cop. He'd jumped over sergeant, lieutenant, captain, and even assistant chief. He was now the chief. Finally, he'd been recognized at a level he deserved. He was given the respect he had earned. He was Chief Prevost. His ego was finally satiated. He had an unmarked car and a secretary, and everyone called him "Chief." Everywhere he went in the small town, he was recognized and catered to. Chief Prevost had arrived in the big leagues and was living large. Well almost.

One day, Chief Prevost was shopping for a few gifts. He just knew that everyone in the store whispered as he walked past, "There goes the Chief of Police." He smiled to himself as he walked past the people in the store. It was obvious to him that they knew who *he* was and that *he* was an important man. He picked out some expensive gifts for family and friends, and filled up the shopping cart while stopping to talk to strangers and introducing himself.

He loved the reaction he received when he mentioned casually in conversation that he was the chief of police, thinking to himself, "That's right bitch. I'm the *man!*" He made small talk with the "commoners" in the store, letting them know that at one time, he had been one of them. Well, at least that's how he saw it.

The truth was that the people he talked to had no idea who he was, nor did they care. *I* have no idea who the chief is of the city I now live in; *I* don't care, and I've been a cop for thirty years. No one cares except the people who work for him.

Chief Prevost strutted around the store with his expensive gifts, and then, when enough people had acknowledged him, he headed to the checkout lines. He swiped his American Express Black card, and smiled at the expression on the clerk's face at the amount he had spent.

Yep. He was a man of means, a man who had earned and deserved your respect.

Karma was about to give the chief a reality check. He walked out of the large retail chain and was approached by the frail and elderly doorman, and asked for his receipt.

Years earlier, retail stores in the US had done research on where the majority of the thefts occurring in their stores originated. They found out, surprisingly, that most theft was internal, meaning that it was committed by employees. One of the most profitable and low-risk ways for employees to steal is for a checker or cashier to fail to scan an item at checkout. A team of professional thieves gets one person hired as a checker at a store, and then the team hits the store over and over, purchasing some items, but not paying for high-priced ones that their "inside man" only pretends to scan. Millions of dollars in profits are lost this way every year.

Several stores developed the "one final check" practice to deal with the issue. After checkout, there is one final check by a trusted, usually older employee. This person checks each receipt to ensure that all the items in a cart have been paid for. This is not to imply that the store doesn't trust its customers; in reality, it doesn't trust its own employees.

On this occasion, the arrogant chief took the request as sign of disrespect. As the chief of police, he should have instantly been recognized. Obviously, he was above the brief inspection. He was not a thief! How could the frail old man not have recognized him immediately?

The fact is that this kind of inspection happens every day at places like Costco, Wal-Mart, and Target stores all over the nation. If the chief had been paying attention during his many part-time jobs instead of sleeping in changing rooms and utility closets, he would've known this.

Chief Prevost at first said no to the request for his receipt and pressed on, ignoring the frail old man. The doorman was not intimidated; he was a WWII veteran and was not about to be treated like a doormat. He sounded the alarm.

Within moments, employees and then a manager surrounded the chief. His arrogance had caught up with him, and he exploded in a tirade of "Fuck you!" and then, "Do you know who the fuck I am?" No—they neither knew nor cared who the fuck he was. It was company policy, and the manager would do whatever it took to keep his job as one of the "common people" the arrogant chief had so recently graced with his presence.

The local police were called when the chief escalated his verbal abuse. Unfortunately for Chief Prevost, he wasn't in "his" city. He was eventually given a citation in lieu of being arrested, and the incident made national news. The store had video of the entire incident, and no matter how the chief tried to paint it as not being his fault, the video didn't leave any doubts.

Just ten short days later, Chief Alan Prevost was relieved of his position by the same city council that had hired him. He made sure to leave them with a small taste of the verbal abuse he'd unleashed on the aging WWII veteran, the guy who'd dared ask for his receipt.

The chief went from his self-imposed status as hero straight to zero in the time it took to inspect a receipt at the door of your local retail store.

CHAPTER TWENTY-TWO

REGGIE STILLS

REGGIE STILLS WAS BORN THE son of a cop, and grew up in the shadow of his father's police uniform. Everywhere he went as a child, people knew his father. Every store they went into to buy groceries, every restaurant they ate in, every movie theater they went to, there was someone who knew his dad and would make a comment or say a thank-you for something his dad had done for them.

That is the reality for cops' kids. Your cop parent is known everywhere and by everyone—usually for doing something good, sometimes for not-so-good things. Always, though, people will come up and talk, and then ask, "Is this your son/daughter?"

Reggie knew what it meant to grow up in a fishbowl with everyone watching your every move. It made him a little more rebellious than most kids in his peer group, and he got into a little more trouble than most.

He was lucky, though. Dads who are cops are not always the best parents. Reggie had a dad who was the exception to that rule. His dad would take him camping and fishing, and was involved in coaching his little league teams.

When Reggie grew older and started to sow some wild oats as a high school-aged kid, his dad sponsored parties at his home. He made sure that kids didn't drive if they were drinking, and when parents asked who would be supervising the party, he would take a day off work and make sure the party was safe for all involved. He was that kind of dad, realistic and grounded. He knew that his son would be drinking and, rather than ignore it and stick his head in the sand and pretend that it wasn't happening, he stepped up.

When Reggie graduated high school, he decided to go into the Marine Corps. His dad hadn't been a Marine, and this made Reggie want to make his own mark and prove himself on his own terms. His dad told me one day while we were on a break getting a drink how proud he was when his son told him that he had enlisted in the Marines. He said that he knew it would be difficult, but he also knew from watching his son that he was strong enough to handle the training and he felt that he would excel. He wasn't disappointed, and when Reggie completed his enlistment and decided to come back home, his father welcomed him.

Reggie returned home with an honorable discharge in hand and a new-found confidence. He'd spent a lot of time thinking about the man that his father was, and when he came home he decided to try his hand at law enforcement as well.

He got a foot in the door by first getting hired by the sheriff's department. Working in corrections gave him a view of the streets from watching and dealing with captured criminals and learning from them on a day-to-day basis. Most cops will tell you that correctional officers make the best street cops, because they live with the arrested criminals of a city for forty hours or more a week. Making sure they are fed three meals and receive medical treatment, and breaking up the inevitable fights that occur, gives you a life experience that few others will ever have. It makes you seasoned in the streets before you ever set foot in a patrol vehicle and start making your own arrests.

Reggie excelled at the job, and in a couple of years tested for the very few open positions in his father's department. He was selected on his second attempt at testing, and passed the police academy easily. Compared to the Marine Corps boot camp, the state police academy was a walk in the park. In no time Reggie was on the streets, working next to his father. His dad couldn't have been more proud.

Father and son were different people. Dad had been married once and stayed married to the same woman for fifty-two years before he died. Reggie was more like me. He couldn't seem to find a woman who could grow with him and deal with the stresses of being a cop's wife. He was married and divorced as many times as I was, maybe more. I never asked. We both worked a lot of overtime trying to stay on top of bills.

Reggie was as gifted on the streets as Billy Webster or Ray Fossum, though he was much more subdued and quiet. He didn't draw a lot of attention to himself or the things that he did.

Reggie applied his Marine training to the job and applied for the department's SWAT team. He was accepted and did well. He excelled at the tactical training, and grasped the concepts better than most of the team leaders. This made him a target, and it wasn't long before he was asked not so politely to leave the team. The powers that be didn't like that he was an independent thinker and quite capable of improvising the tactics they thought of as carved in stone. They were black-and-white thinkers, while Reggie saw the world in shades of grey.

Reggie left the team and quietly disappeared onto the midnight shift, where the target that always seemed to be present on the back of his head was less visible to others. Reggie layed low, did his job at night, and like his father, did a great job of taking care of his kids. He coached them at soccer and frequently would come to briefing before shift beaming at how well his little girls had done at their games.

He was seriously much more proud of what his girls did in sports and school than I ever saw him at anything he did at work. He accomplished a lot in the streets, but nothing brought him the joy he experienced coaching and watching his girls. It would be no exaggeration to say there were tears in his eyes more than once while he bragged about them. He was a very proud father. We both were—and like me, he was a horrible husband.

Reggie decided to take a turn in the floundering gang unit and made a huge impact there. He gathered intelligence on the local gangs in a manner that had never been seen or attempted before. To say that he had a gift was an understatement. He could find out what had happened during a particular incident in very short order. Unlike the previous gang detectives, he listened to everyone, gang members and cops alike. He was able to put some amazingly difficult cases together just by doing what he did best: listening and being an exceptional cop.

Reggie and I rolled through divorces, one after another, and would often joke in a painful way about our fucked-up lives. We each would meet our soul mates soon enough, but not yet.

Reggie finally met what he thought was the perfect woman one night in the emergency room. He was bringing in the latest drunk, or perhaps he was called up there on the latest stabbing or shooting victim to have been dumped off at the emergency room doors. I don't really know, but I do know that is where he met the dark-eyed nurse. She was a beauty, seriously, and I envied him. She was married, and her marriage was going to shit, as was Reggie's.

Cops and emergency room nurses live life without the rose-colored glasses that most of us take for granted. The rest of us read in the paper about one-tenth of the horrors that really go on in the streets. You might read about one rape that occurred the previous night, or one fatal crash. Cops and emergency room nurses see all of it—not just the single case that gets printed but the dozens that don't.

They don't just read about it, they live it. The screams of the helpless and wounded in pain: the smell of blood, brains, and shit of the near-dead and dying. They see and experience it all and come back the next night for the next installment of what the rest of us rarely even realize is going on, every day, all day long.

Reggie was sitting in a waiting room when the nurse came in. Beautiful as ever, she looked at Reggie and smiled. There was something in her eyes that night that made the smile look more like a grimace of pain than a greeting. Reggie noticed it immediately, and started to talk to her. He was genuinely concerned, wondering if she was okay. The two groups, cops and nurses, spar a lot, but also genuinely care about each other. There is no one else in their worlds who understands what they see and the toll it takes.

Reggie talked to her while she did her work of checking blood pressure and assessing a patient's health. He watched like only a good cop can, noticing little changes in the facial expressions and posture that clue you in that something isn't right. Later, he made a point out of coming back up when he knew she would be at lunch. He sat down uninvited, again as only a cop will, and began to coax the nurse to talk to him.

In a few minutes, the normally hard-as-stone emergency room nurse was in tears. She told him of her disastrous marriage and her fear that she would be alone. Then she dropped the bomb on him: she was addicted to pain pills and had been stealing them from the emergency room. She admitted that she couldn't sleep without them. The nightmares of the damaged bodies she saw night in and night out made sleep impossible without the prescription drugs she skimmed from the emergency room pharmacy.

She had worked her way through nursing school with no scholarship and no assistance. It was hard, but it had been her dream to be a nurse and to make a difference. Now she felt like it was all falling apart. Her job as a nurse, her marriage, basically her entire life, it was all going to shit because of the addiction. Reggie listened carefully.

Cops talk to people who are at their wits' end every day. They spill their guts to cops much like a person might to a priest. It is a cleansing moment, I suppose, to release all of the fears and emotion to someone you feel you can trust. Good cops have an innate knack for knowing when to push, and when to sit in silence and listen, and Reggie was an excellent cop.

He sat and listened till she was done; relieved and exhausted, she thanked him for listening. He gave her his cell phone number and told her to call anytime, day or night, if she needed to talk. They parted ways that day and the hook was set.

To this day I am really glad she talked to him and not me.

Reggie took more and more of the beautiful nurse's burdens on his shoulders. He was going through his own painful divorce, and was busy keeping his kids' lives together in the daytime. Meanwhile, he helped the emergency room nurse out as much as he could. Eventually she was caught stealing from the emergency room pharmacy, and was put on a probation for addiction. She was exceptional as a nurse, and the hospital administration hoped that she would be able to be salvaged.

They decided to give her one chance at proving herself worthy of their trust. She had to complete a drug rehab program, and an extended probation period. She had to submit to random drug tests, and couldn't work as a nurse until she had completed the probation, rehab program, and drug tests. The administration made it painfully clear that one slip, and she was done in the profession. Period.

She took a considerable cut in pay, her failing marriage ended, and she had to sell her home and car. She had nowhere to go, and in steps Reggie. Like I said, the hook was set; he had no idea of the shit storm he was stepping into.

The beautiful nurse was playing him like she owned him, which she pretty much did. She did get an apartment in the central city, living next to drug dealers and gang members, calling Reggie every time a gunshot went off in the streets. Reggie eventually moved her into his house after the brief show of her "independence." Over a period of about a year and a half, they went from separate bedrooms to the same bed, and later they were married.

Reggie kept her toeing the line, and she eventually did get her job back. She was back in the emergency room, working with her peers and feeling good about herself again. Reggie, too, was proud of the change in her, and the strength she had shown. He felt that he finally had a woman who had enough life experience to understand his life and the things he saw. When he saw that she truly did understand what he was experiencing, it made him feel less isolated and alone when he talked about things that happened at work. Life was good for both of them, and they both felt like they were finally on the right track.

One day Reggie came home from work, and a few minutes later his new wife also came home. She was talking to him about her day when the warning bells started to chime in the back of his head. As he listened, he picked up on very subtle changes in her pronunciation of more complex words as she spoke.

He realized she was high as hell. He watched and listened silently as she gradually became worse. The changes were minor, and could have been due to fatigue, but Reggie knew the difference. Once you have been a cop for a while you don't miss much.

Sometimes you really do wish you could suppress the "cop radar" and just live in ignorance like the rest of the world. There is nothing like listening to someone you care about lie through her fucking teeth and tell you, "Oh no, honey, I was with my girlfriends," or "No, I was held over late at work," when you can see in her eyes that she's just left her latest man-on-the-side. In Reggie's case, what his wife's lies were covering was the fact that she was back to being an addict.

Reggie had a few faults himself; we all do. Perhaps being too loyal was one. He couldn't walk away from the beautiful nurse. He had watched over and over on the street as addicts destroyed the lives of the people who loved them. He thought, or perhaps he just hoped, that he could make this be the exception.

He tried to work with his wife and be there for her. Eventually, though, she convinced him that she couldn't get through the day without at least some of the pain pills.

He knew that she would lose her job when she was caught. It was just a matter of time before the emergency room found the discrepancies in the nightly count of each pain pill they issued.

Reggie decided that if he could buy his wife some time, maybe he could get her sober through intervention. I know that, in hindsight, it seems stupid, but honestly, I cannot fault him for trying.

Reggie started to buy pain pills on line from Mexico and had them shipped to the U.S. to a post office box he had purchased. He hoped to wean his wife off of the pills slowly and maybe return to the previously happy life that they had made for themselves.

It did work for a while—until one day the DEA showed up at the police department.

To give Reggie credit, he didn't lie about the incident, and did his best to explain his situation. But it didn't matter. The DEA saw him as a dealer providing an addict with a controlled substance. His career as a cop was over.

That wouldn't have been so bad, really. He loved his wife, and he had his kids. A new job and a new beginning can sometimes be good things. His wife, however, was nowhere near as committed to their marriage as he was. She made a deal with prosecutors to testify against him in exchange for lesser charges. She looked out for number one as she always had, and left him speechless in the hallways of the courthouse. Alone, unemployed and now a convicted felon.

CHAPTER TWENTY-THREE
ROY GREY

ROY GREY WAS AN OLD-SCHOOL cop. He started on the force in the early 70s and made his way to detective earlier than most cops. He was the epitome of that old saying in the cop world, "You have to have been there to know how to get there." The big difference in Roy's case was that he never really left "there."

He could be professional in public when he needed to be, wearing a suit and tie, wing tips, and cufflinks. This was a ruse, however. Roy came from the old school, the school that believed confessions needed to be beaten out of a suspect, and that the more difficult the confession was to get, the more brutal the beating needed to be.

He arrived in the detectives' unit a few months before a brutal crime occurred in the city. It was the 70s, and LSD was rampant on the streets. A couple of members of the military got a hold of some LSD and got really high. They then went into a local business, and proceeded to torture and rape the employees. They locked the doors and pretty much went to town on the employees and a couple of people who were unlucky enough to have been in the place. After they were done, they left what was remaining of the maimed and tortured people there for the cops to find. The case received national attention. The murders were horrific, and the few survivors were permanently injured.

I was a child at the time, and I remember that the entire city walked in fear until the suspects were identified and caught. Everyone breathed a sigh of relief. Roy had a hand in their capture and then their conviction. Years later, when I joined that same police department, the case was still whispered about in the hallways.

Some cases are like that. They seem to have a life of their own and never die. Every cop has a case that haunts him or her, whether they are closed with an arrest and conviction or not. This case haunted the entire city for years, it was that horrific.

Fast forward several years, and Roy was out at night. He was not officially on duty but, like most cops, he was never really off duty. He always had his badge and gun, and carried them with him.

Roy had a habit of picking fights with anyone who caught his eye. He liked to find guys who were a little bit cocky, maybe a bit street-wise—wannabe thugs. He hoped they would mistake his age and professional dress as signs of weakness. He would confront them in an aggressive and condescending tone. When they finally had enough of his abuse and called him on it, he would beat the hell out of them. Then, after he had beaten them into submission, he would let them know that he was a cop, flashing his badge and making sure they knew not to report the incident. He would give the victim a break this time and not arrest him. Lucky break for the guy that he was in a generous mood.

This went on frequently, and he never was caught. This is what he did for entertainment. Rumors floated around the department, and as people in the city talked to the cops they knew about the "rogue cop" who would deliver beatings and then disappear. For all I know, he could have been the cop who beat the hell out of Scott Preston when Scott was at the ripe old age of six or seven.

One night Roy was out prowling, looking for the next cocky thug who needed one of his famous reality checks. He ran into a couple of guys, nineteen or twenty years old, who were in a dark parking lot— "long hairs," as Roy called the young men at that time. I can see him thinking of them as hippies, which was his frame of reference for a time period that had already passed him by.

Roy pulled up and confronted the "hippies." He started a practiced and well-worn speech that always got things warmed up quickly. The sooner the fight began, the better, from Roy's perspective.

Tonight would be different, however. Roy started the fight as usual, and things were going along as planned. He was delivering a pretty substantial beating to the guy he had selected when things took a turn for the worse.

I know this because the guy whom Roy chose to beat up that night was my next-door neighbor's boyfriend. He was normally a quiet guy. Yes, he definitely had long hair, but unknown to Roy, he was an awesome fighter.

This guy beat the hell out of Roy. To emphasize the point that he had beat Roy's ass soundly, he slammed Roy's head onto the concrete a couple of times. This ended up causing some permanent brain damage to the now-veteran cop. The number one rule on the street is that there is always someone who can beat your ass, no matter how bad you think you are. Roy learned that lesson the hard way after delivering many unwarranted and unnecessary beatings himself.

Roy could not believe that he had been beaten, and, perhaps to save face, he saw to it that charges were filed against the "long hair." The courts saw through Roy's bullshit claims, and even a "long hair" has a right to be heard in court. The courts sided with the "long hair", and Roy's complaint was dismissed.

Roy had a couple of kids whom he parented as brutally and as mercilessly as he patrolled. His children grew up personally experiencing the old saying, "spare the rod, spoil the child." Roy was determined that his children would not be spoiled, and he never "spared the rod," to the point of excess. They grew up tough and hard, fighting as often as their angry father.

I first arrested Roy's eldest son after I had been with the department for about two years. He was involved in an aggravated assault. He was clearly in the wrong, and when I put him in my car, the first thing out of his mouth was, "Do you know who my dad is? You will severely regret this." He then he spewed out a train of insults, and spit on my face. It was a pleasure to book him into jail, screaming and obviously terrified. As I left the jail, I watched him screaming into a telephone, "Dad, I'm in jail! Get me the FUCK out of here now!"

Roy did get him out of jail that night, and from then on, we were enemies. He never said a word to me. He would not go to lunch if I were present, and if I showed up to eat with the other cops and he was there, he would leave. Interesting thing happened though: several of the veterans patted me on the back and praised me for the arrest.

They said that Roy had bullied his way around the department long enough, and it was about time someone arrested his fucked-up kids. They said that Roy had protected them from the cops for years. My case was solid, and Roy's kid was convicted. Roy was livid.

I watched Roy for a few more years before he finally retired. His brain damage from the fight with my neighbor's boyfriend was obvious. He had a difficult time writing reports, and a small group of senior patrolmen would always double-check his paperwork, looking for errors before he turned them in.

I kept an eye out for his kid, as I could tell that he would be a continuing problem in the city. We crossed paths a few times, and it was always memorable. He no longer mentioned his cop father when he was arrested. He would always spit, however. Nice guy.

Several years later, I saw that Roy's son had been arrested for murdering his wife. He had learned the lessons of his brutal childhood well. He beat his wife to death in an argument, and the neighbors had called the cops. There would be no calling Roy to get out of jail this time. A few weeks after the arrest, Roy's son killed himself in jail. He did not want to spend the rest of his life in prison as the son of a cop. His life would have been unpleasant at best.

To me, Roy is perhaps one of the saddest stories in this book. He was a hero in the 70s, following the arrest and conviction of two nationally known murderers. His brutal life took its toll on his family. I wouldn't want to be in his shoes for anything.

A SPECIAL PREVIEW OF

CURBCHEK

ZACH FORTIER

SKIDMARK

"SKIDMARK" WAS THE COP'S NICKNAME; his real name was Skidlaski. Skidmark was what we called him when we thought about him—which wasn't often. It wasn't because he smelled bad (which he did); we just had to consider him because he made our jobs more difficult.

He had zero common sense, and no feel for the street. He was one of those guys who thought he knew more than everyone else, and wouldn't listen to anyone. My first memory of him is him pulling over a vehicle in a grocery store parking lot so that lots of people could see him. He'd been assigned to my area, so I had to take some calls with him.

It was Christmas Eve, and it's an unwritten rule among us cops that Christmas is hands-off: no bullshit tickets, no arrests unless it's absolutely necessary and only when there's no other choice. We'd talk about it in briefing, with no objections from the sergeants.

So Skidmark pulled over this vehicle and started running the occupants. The son of a bitch was digging for warrants—and he'd already violated the rules just by stopping them.

I drove past to see that he had pulled over this station wagon full of wrapped presents with three scared little kids in the back; as I drove off, Skidmark waved at me as I passed like he was thanking me for checking on him. I left this bullshit scene and listened for the outcome of the stop on the radio: the plates on the station wagon had expired, and the mother was driving on an expired license.

Skidmark called for a wrecker and impounded the car with the gifts inside; he actually put the kids and the mom on the street on Christmas

Eve. He did at least call someone to come pick them up after giving her a ticket. A regular St. Dick he was.

From that point on, I was done with him. I cancelled him on every call; I wouldn't work with him. He had a really fucked-up way of seeing the world, which I couldn't understand and didn't want to.

I became one of his most outspoken opponents in the department and on the street. I started to hear from people in the area where we worked about how poorly he treated everyone, and how they really didn't like him and couldn't talk to him, which was pretty much unraveling everything the rest of us had worked so damned hard to establish; it was blowing relationships and eroding all the trust that we were trying to build. He was constantly making our jobs harder by being such a horse's ass. He was a real cheese dick.

One night, Skidmark had arrested a guy for drinking beer in one of the city parks. He felt like he was cleaning up the area by arresting everyone for anything he could think of, anytime they moved; like I said, he had no feel for the street.

We overlooked a lot of smaller crimes because we needed the cooperation of the residents of the city to land the bigger fish. Maybe you just mentioned the statute of limitations that would allow us to file the charges any time in the next two to four years, whatever it was; maybe you didn't mention it at all if you didn't need to. Inner-city dwellers knew about how the criminal justice system worked as well as we did.

Skidmark couldn't grasp this concept, though, and he arrested everyone for even the slightest of violations in order to pump up his stats. In some misguided attempt to break up cliques in the department, management had come up with a shift-bid system in which the highest performers on each squad could pick their shifts for the following year. They called it the golden squad; we called it the golden shower squad. It didn't work, but it lasted for a long, long time.

New guys like Skidmark saw this as a way to get better shifts without having to pay their dues on the street like all the rest of us had. He wanted to get off the graveyard shift as soon as possible; I, on the other hand, loved "graves," particularly since my latest marriage was coming undone. It allowed me to avoid the wife and spend time with my kids.

On this particular day, Skidmark had arrested this guy for drinking in the park; he had done so under an obscure ordinance meant to help us keep the parks clear of drunks, not common citizens sharing a few beers while barbecuing.

The guy Skidmark arrested was pissed off, and Skidmark was talking shit to him as he was taking him to his car, telling the guy what a waste of a human being he was. He handcuffed him, put him in the car, seat-belted him in, and locked the door. He then left to go back to the park to arrest a couple more guys he saw drinking there.

This was really stupid, not to mention a safety problem, creating real potential for a violent cluster; any cop who's worked the streets will tell you that. You don't load up your car with drunks to take to jail just so you can get stats.

Skidmark arrested another guy and brought him back to his car—only to find it empty, with the passenger door wide open; the first guy had unlocked the car and run off with his handcuffs. The cuffs were your personal property back then. We had to buy them, and of course Skidmark always carried a lot of them.

He jumped on the radio, screaming for backup because he had an escaped prisoner. I didn't move; I just listened to the shit storm unfold, and shook my head. Several units looked for the guy for hours, but couldn't find him. How impressive is that: shaking people down for details on the guy who stole an officer's cuffs?

I just stayed out of it. I didn't want anyone on the street to see me with this dickhead, or associate me with helping him. He finally gave up and took the rest of his catch to jail, then bitched for days about "that piece of shit who stole my cuffs" and how he'd get even. Gave his pitiful little life direction, I guess.

About a week went by, and I got a call to meet a woman I knew at her home. When I showed up, she was sitting on the front porch with her son and daughter. She said that she wanted me to hear what her son had to say.

He was just a kid, maybe 19 or 20. I listened, and he told me about how he was arrested and had escaped with the officer's handcuffs. It was Skidmark's escaped bad guy! My reaction wasn't what he expected. The kid was all tense and edgy, and I think he expected to get hit or take a beating; instead, I started to laugh—and laugh hard!

"Really? That was you?" I asked.

He said that it was, and he recounted how Skidmark—he didn't know it was Skidmark, of course; he called him "Officer Cheesedick" (quite funny, really)—made him angry talking down to him, so after he was left in the car, he felt it was his duty to try to escape. He also described how Skidmark had a distinctive odor, and was fat, and wheezed. The kid said, "I felt like a bitch going down without fighting this guy."

I was laughing really hard by now at his descriptions, amazed that it reflected almost exactly how most of Skidmark's fellow officers felt about him. His mother, however, wasn't happy, and didn't see the humor in it; she didn't want her son to feel that this was acceptable behavior.

To hell with that. I explained that "Skidmark" was his nickname and that he was exactly what her son had described—and although I didn't endorse his escape, I did understand it.

She asked, "What are you going to do now?"

I looked at the son and said, "Well, that's up to you. I don't wanna lose *my* cuffs. If you're gonna run, have at it, man. Go!"

He didn't move. I told him that if he went with me, he'd go willingly, then gave him my cuffs and told him to put them on. His jaw dropped. He asked if I was serious.

"Yeah man," I said. "You put them on, then you can show me how you got out of Skidmark's car."

He liked that idea. He was proud of the fact that he'd escaped. He even put the cuffs on behind his back. I took him to the car, buckled him in, locked the door, and said, "Go!"

He was out in 15 seconds. I was seriously impressed with his method—which, for obvious reasons, I won't reveal. I sat there with him and, with his help, figured out a way to thwart his escape. We then laughed and joked, talking and exchanging ideas.

Then I let him tell his mom goodbye, took him to jail, and booked him on the warrant of the escape charge against him. I told him that Skidmark was on duty that night. "He's gonna want to come talk shit to you. The cuffs you took were his favorite set", I said.

"You don't still have them, do you?" I asked. He said no, that he'd cut them off and thrown them away.

I called Skidmark on the radio and told him that his escapee had been booked into jail. He replied that he was on his way to the jail; for him, this was personal.

I warned the kid about him being on his way, then left. Nothing ever came of it. Skidmark continued doing his thing; I just made a point of not working with him.

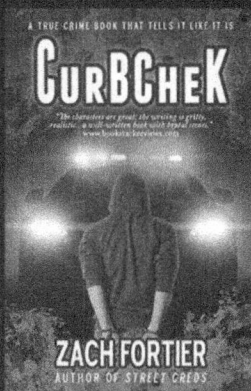

ABOUT THE AUTHOR
ZACH FORTIER

ZACH FORTIER WAS A POLICE officer for over 30 years specializing in K-9, SWAT, gang, domestic violence, and sex crimes as an investigator. He has written three books about police work. The first book, *CurbChek,* is a case-by-case account of the streets as he worked them from the start of his career. The second book, *Street Creds*, details the time he spent in a gang task force and the cases that occurred. The third book, *CurbChek Reload*, is by far the most gritty. The author is dangerously damaged, suffering from post-traumatic stress syndrome (PTSD) and the day-to-day violence of working the street. *Hero To Zero,* his fourth book, details the incredibly talented cops that he worked with but ended up going down in flames. Some ended up in prison and one on the FBI's ten most wanted list.

If you are looking for gritty, true crime stories, be sure to check out all of Zach Fortier's novels.

www.ingramcontent.com/pod-product-compliance
Lightning Source LLC
Chambersburg PA
CBHW032001040426
42448CB00006B/442